CRAZY PRAYERS
FOR
COOL KIDS

p

CRAZY JOKES
For
COOL KIDS

This is a Parragon Book
This edition published in 2004

Parragon
Queen Street House
4 Queen Street
Bath BA1 1HE, UK

Produced by Magpie Books, an imprint of
Constable & Robinson Ltd, London

ISBN 1-40542-654-3

A copy of the British Library Cataloguing-in-Publication Data
is available from the British Library

Printed and bound in the EC

Contents

Contents Continued

Introduction

What kind of person thinks his bath is
electric because it has a plug? An idiot,
that's who. And as you will learn from
these pages there are an awful lot of
them about doing some pretty crazy
things. But just beware: word tricks
can make you or a friend look a bit
of a fool too . . .

Creatures Great and Small

A woodpecker was pecking a hole in a tree. All of a sudden a flash of lightning struck the tree to the ground. The woodpecker looked bemused for a moment and then said: "Gee, I guess I don't know my own strength."

What do you get if you cross a hedgehog with a giraffe?
A long-necked toothbrush.

There was once a puppy called May who loved to pick quarrels with animals who were bigger than she was. One day she argued with a lion. The next day was the first of June.
Why? Because that was the end of May!

What kind of cats love water?
Octopusses.

Why does a stork stand on one leg?
Because it would fall over if it lifted the
other one.

First flea: You don't look too well.
Second flea: I'm not really feeling up to
scratch.

My dog saw a sign that said: "Wet Paint" –
so he did!

What's a porcupine's favourite food?
Prickled onions.

My dog is a nuisance. He chases everyone on a bicycle. What can I do?
Take his bike away.

What's an American cat's favourite car?
A Catillac.

What's black and white and makes a lot of noise?
A zebra with a set of drums.

What is a snail?
A slug with a crash helmet.

What should you do if you find a gorilla sitting at your school desk?
Sit somewhere else.

What did the stupid ghost call his pet tiger?
Spot.

Teacher: Who can tell me what geese eat?
Paul: Er, gooseberries, Sir?

Mary had a bionic cow,
It lived on safety pins.
And every time she milked that cow
The milk came out in tins.

Why should a school not be near a chicken farm?
To avoid the pupils overhearing fowl language.

Teacher: Martin, put some more water in the fish tank.
Martin: But, Sir, they haven't drunk the water I gave them yesterday.

What were the only creatures not to go into the Ark in pairs?
Maggots. They went in an apple.

What do you get if you pour hot water down a rabbit hole?
Hot cross bunnies!

What do you get if you cross a galaxy with a toad?
Star Warts.

On which side does a chicken have the most feathers?
On the outside.

Which bird is always out of breath?
A puffin.

What's the best thing to give a seasick elephant?
Plenty of room.

What sort of fish performs surgical operations?
A sturgeon.

Just before the Ark set sail, Noah saw his two sons fishing over the side. "Go easy on the bait, lads," he said. "Remember I've only got two worms."

What's a twip?
What a wabbit calls a twain ride!

Baby skunk: But, Mum, why can't I have a chemistry set for my birthday?
Mother: Because it would stink the house out, that's why.

Waiter, waiter, there's a dead beetle in my gravy.
Yes, sir. Beetles are terrible swimmers.

Keith: Our teacher's an old bat.
Kevin: You mean he's bad-tempered?
Keith: Not only that, he hangs around us all the time.

A teacher took her class for a walk in the country, and Susie found a grass snake. "Come quickly, Miss," she called, "here's a tail without a body!"

The Stock Market is a place where sheep and cattle are sold.

How do you catch a squirrel?
Climb up a tree and act like a nut.

Which animals do you have to beware of when you take exams?
Cheetahs.

Why did the elephant paint her head yellow?
To see if blondes really do have more fun.

How many skunks does it take to make a big stink?
A phew!

What was the fly doing in the alphabet soup?
Learning to spell.

What happened when the headmistress's poodle swallowed a roll of film?
Nothing serious developed.

What did the neurotic pig say to the
farmer?
You take me for grunted.

What did the beaver say to the tree?
It sure is good to gnaw you.

Why don't centipedes play football?
Because by the time they've got their
boots on it's time to go home.

What's the difference between a coyote
and a flea?
One howls on the prairie, and the other
prowls on the hairy.

Donald: My canary died of flu.
Dora: I didn't know canaries got flu.
Donald: Mine flew into a car.

How do fleas travel from place to place?
By itch-hiking.

What do you get if you cross a yeti with a kangaroo?
A fur coat with big pockets.

What do you get if you cross a cow and a camel?
Lumpy milkshakes!

What do you get if you cross a sheep-dog
and a bunch of daisies?
Collie-flowers!

What do you get if you cross a zebra and a
donkey?
A zeedonk.

What do you get if you cross a sheep and a
rainstorm?
A wet blanket.

What do you get if you cross a vampire
with a flea?
Lots of very worried dogs.

There were two mosquitoes watching blood donors giving their blood. "It's not fair," said one to the other. "They're happy to lie down and let someone drain a pint of blood, but if we zoomed down for a quick nip, they'd do their best to kill us."

An elephant ran away from a circus and ended up in a little old lady's back garden. The lady had never seen an elephant before, so she rang the police.

"Please come quickly," she said to the policeman who answered the phone.

"There's a strange looking animal in my garden picking up cabbages with its tail."

"What's it doing with them?" asked the policeman.

"If I told you," said the old lady, "you'd never believe me!"

What do you get if you cross a centipede
and a parrot?
A walkie-talkie.

Two caterpillars were crawling along a twig
when a butterfly flew by. "You know," said
one caterpillar to the other, "when I grow
up, you'll never get me in one of those
things."

What dog smells of onions?
A hot dog.

What lies on the ground 100 feet up in the
air and smells?
A dead centipede.

What did the grape do when the elephant sat on it?
It let out a little wine.

What do you call a flea that lives in an idiot's ear?
A space invader.

What do ants take when they are ill?
Antibiotics.

Who conquered half the world, laying eggs along the way?
Attila the Hen.

Why was the young kangaroo thrown out
by his mother?
For smoking in bed.

When is it bad luck to be followed by a
black cat?
When you're a mouse.

The psychiatrist was surprised to see a tortoise come into his office. "What can I do for you, Mr Tortoise?" asked the psychiatrist.

"I'm terribly shy, doctor," said the tortoise, "I want you to cure me of that."

"No problem. I'll soon have you out of your shell."

Two fish were swimming in a stream when it began to rain. "Quick," said one fish to the other, "let's swim under that bridge, otherwise we'll get wet!"

What do you get if you cross an owl with a vampire?

A bird that's ugly but doesn't give a hoot.

"Who's been eating my porridge?"
squeaked Baby Bear.
"Who's been eating my porridge?" cried
Mother Bear.
"Burp!" said Father Bear.

Why are skunks always arguing?
'Cos they like to raise a stink.

If twenty dogs run after one dog, what
time is it?
Twenty after one.

Rabbits can multipy – but only a snake can
be an adder.

How did Noah see to the animals in the
Ark?
By flood-lighting.

What swings through trees and is very
dangerous?
A chimpanzee with a machine-gun.

What has four legs, whiskers, a tail, and
flies?
A dead cat.

Have you ever seen a man-eating tiger?
No, but in the café next door I once saw a
man eating chicken!

First cat: How did you get on in the milk-drinking contest?
Second cat: Oh, I won by six laps!

A man who bought a dog took it back, complaining that it made a mess all over the house. "I thought you said it was house-trained," he moaned.
"So it is," said the previous owner. "It won't go anywhere else."

Sign in shop window:
FOR SALE Pedigree bulldog. House-trained. Eats anything. Very fond of children.

Why couldn't the butterfly go to the dance?
Because it was a moth-ball.

What do you get if you cross a flea with a rabbit?
Bugs Bunny.

What do you get if you cross a crocodile with a flower?
I don't know, but I'm not going to smell it.

What do you call a multi-storey pig-pen?
A styscraper.

How can you tell if an elephant has been sleeping in your bed?
The sheets are wrinkled and the bed smells of peanuts.

Did you hear about the boy who sat under a cow?
He got a pat on the head.

Why do elephants have flat feet?
From jumping out of tall trees.

Is the squirt from an elephant's trunk very powerful?
Of course – a jumbo jet can keep 500 people in the air for hours at a time.

How do you make an elephant sandwich?
First of all you get a very large loaf . . .

What has two tails, two trunks and five
legs?
An elephant with spare parts.

Mean and Nasty Jokes

The garbage men were just about to leave the street when a woman came running out of the house carrying some cardboard boxes.

"Am I too late for the garbage?" she called.

"No, lady," replied one of the men. "Jump right in!"

A woman woke her husband in the middle of the night. "There's a burglar downstairs eating the cake that I made this morning."

"Who shall I call," her husband said, "Police or ambulance?"

Girl: Did you like that cake Mrs Jones?

Mrs Jones: Yes, very much.

Girl: That's funny. My mum said you didn't have any taste.

Fred: I was sorry to hear that your mother-in-law had died. What was the complaint?

Ted: We haven't had any yet.

When you leave school, you should become a bone specialist. You've certainly got the head for it.

My Auntie Maud had so many candles on her last birthday cake that all her party guests got sunburnt.

When Wally Witherspoon proposed to his girlfriend she said:
"I love the simple things in life, Wally, but I don't want one of them for a husband."

Two friends were discussing the latest scandalous revelations about a Hollywood actress.
"They say she likes her latest husband so much she's decided to keep him for another month," said one to the other.

Roger was in a very full bus when a fat woman opposite said, "If you were a gentleman, young man, you'd stand up and let someone else sit down."

"And if you were a lady," replied Roger, "you'd stand up and let four people sit down."

My son's just received a scholarship to medical school – but they don't want him while he's alive.

My mother uses lemon juice for her complexion. Maybe that is why she always looks so sour.

My Auntie Mabel has got so many double chins it looks like she is peering over a pile of crumpets.

Chuck: Do you have holes in your underpants?
Teacher: No, of course not.
Chuck: Then how do you get your feet through?

My girlfriend talks so much that when she goes on holiday, she has to spread suntan lotion on her tongue.

At my piano teacher's last performance the audience cheered and cheered. The piano was locked!

A school inspector was talking to a pupil. "How many teachers work in this school?" he asked.
"Only about half of them, I reckon," replied the pupil.

Father: Would you like me to help you with your homework?
Son: No thanks, I'd rather get it wrong by myself.

I wouldn't say our English teacher is fat, but when she got on a Speak Your Weight machine it surrendered.

Rob: I must rush home and cut the lawn.
Teacher: Did your father promise you something if you cut it?
Rob: No, he promised me something if I didn't!

She's such a gossip she tells you what you were going to say to her before you have the chance to tell her.

I have two noses, three eyes and only one ear. What am I?
Very ugly.

Mrs Broadbeam: Now, remember, children, travel is very good for you. It broadens the mind.
Sarah, muttering: If you're anything to go by, that's not all it broadens!

Why is a caretaker nothing like Robinson Crusoe?
Because Robinson Crusoe got all his work done by Friday.

"Did you see him?" asked the policeman. "No," said Mrs Blenkinsop, "but I'd know that laugh anywhere."

What do you get if you pour boiling water down a rabbit hole?
Hot cross bunnies.

I can't get over that new beard of yours. It makes your face look just like a busted sofa.

Henry: I'd like to learn to play a drum, Sir.
Music teacher: Beat it!

Yes, I do like your dress – but isn't it a little early for Hallowe'en?

You must think I'm a perfect idiot.
No, you're not perfect.

Soprano at concert: And what would you like me to sing next?

Member of audience: Do you know "Old Man River"?

Soprano: Er, yes.

Member of audience: Well go jump in it.

I don't care who you are, get those reindeer off my roof.

I don't know what it is that makes you stupid but whatever it is, it works.

My dad is rather tired this morning. Last night he dreamed he was working.

Wife: Shall I give that tramp one of my cakes?
Husband: Why, what harm has he ever done us?

My uncle spent a fortune on deodorants before he found out that people didn't like him anyway.

What is small, pink, wrinkly, and belongs to Grandpa?
Grandma.

Why do gorillas have big nostrils?
Because they have big fingers.

Why don't you go home and brush up on your ignorance?

How does your head feel today?
As good as new.
It should be as good as new – it's never been used.

My uncle must be the meanest man in the world. He recently found a crutch – then he broke his leg so he could use it.

I've got a good idea.
Must be beginner's luck.

I reckon Mum must be at least 30 years old – I counted the rings under her eyes.

Woman: If you were my husband, I'd poison your coffee.
Man: And if you were my wife, I'd drink it.

Visitor: You're very quiet, Jennifer.
Jennifer: Well, my mum gave me 10 pence not to say anything about your red nose.

Mum! There's a man at the door collecting for the Old Folks' Home. Shall I give him Grandma?

I've just finished painting your portrait.
There, don't you think it looks like you?
Er . . . well . . . it probably looks better
from a distance.
"I told you it was like you!"

The new office-boy came into his boss's
office and said, "I think you're wanted on
the phone, sir."
"What d'you mean, you think?" demanded
the boss.
"Well, sir, the phone rang, I answered it
and a voice said, 'Is that you, you old
fool?'"

Billy: I never had a sled when I was a kid.
We were too poor.
Milly, feeling sorry for him: What a shame!
What did you do when it snowed?
Billy: Slid down the hills on my cousin.

Do you think, Professor, that my wife
should take up the piano as a career?
No, I think she should put down the lid as a
favor.

Why did you refuse to marry Richard,
Tessa?
'Cos he said he would die if I didn't and I'm
just curious.

My Peter keeps telling everyone he's going to marry the most beautiful girl in the world.
What a shame! And after all the time you've been engaged!

Doctor Sawbones speaking.
Oh, doctor, my wife's just dislocated her jaw. Can you come over in, say, three or four weeks time?

"How should I have played that last shot?" the bad golfer asked his partner.
"Under an assumed name."

May I go swimming, Mummy?
No, you may not. There are sharks here.
But Daddy's swimming.
He's insured.

Alfie had been listening to his sister
practice her singing. "Sis," he said, "I wish
you'd sing Christmas carols."
"That's nice of you Alfie," she said, "why?"
"Then I'd only have to hear you once a
year!"

Nurse: Doctor, there's an invisible man in
the waiting-room.
Doctor: Tell him I can't see him.

A naughty child was irritating all the passengers on the flight from London to New York. Finally, one man could stand it no longer. "Hey kid," he shouted, "why don't you go outside and play?"

A scoutmaster asked one of his troop what good deed he had done for the day. "Well Skip," said the scout. "Mum had only one dose of castor oil left, so I let my baby brother have it."

Accountant: I'm having trouble sleeping – any suggestions?
Doctor: Have you tried counting sheep?

The apprentice electrician was on his first job. "Take hold of those two wires, Alex," said his master, "and rub them together." Alex did as he was bid, and his master said, "Do you feel anything?"

"No," said Alex.

"That's good – so don't touch those other two wires or you'll get a nasty shock!"

A rather stern aunt had been staying with Sharon's parents, and one day she said to the little girl, "Well, Sharon, I'm going tomorrow. Are you sorry?"

"Oh yes, Auntie," replied Sharon. "I thought you were going today."

Mr Brown: I hate to tell you, but your wife just fell in the wishing well.
Mr Smith: It works!

Did you hear about the woman who was so ugly she could make yogurt by staring at a pint of milk for an hour?

"Some girls think I'm handsome," said the young Romeo, "and some girls think I'm ugly. What do you think, Sheila?"
"A bit of both. Pretty ugly."

You're ugly!
And you're drunk!
Yes, but in the morning I'll be sober!

I don't think these photographs you've
taken do me justice.
You don't want justice – you want mercy!

Food and
Physical Jokes

Jane's father decided to take all the family out to a restaurant for a meal. As he'd spent quite a lot of money for the meal he said to the waiter, "Could I have a bag to take the leftovers home for the dog?"

"Gosh!" exclaimed Jane, "are we getting a dog?"

A fat girl went into a café and ordered two slices of apple pie with four scoops of ice cream covered with lashings of raspberry sauce and piles of chopped nuts. "Would you like a cherry on the top?" asked the waitress.

"No, thanks," said the girl, "I'm on a diet."

Why is it that when I stand on my head the blood rushes to my head but when I stand on my feet the blood doesn't rush to my feet?
Your feet aren't empty.

Mum: Eat up your roast beef, it's full of iron.
Dottie: No wonder it's so tough.

A woman telephoned her local newspaper to let them know that she had just given birth to eighteen children. The reporter didn't quite hear the message and said, "Would you repeat that?"
"Not if I can help it," replied the woman.

Neil: I've changed my mind.
Jim: About time, too. Does the new one work any better?

You should get a job in the meteorology office.
Why?
Because you're an expert on wind.

That boy is so dirty, the only time he washes his ears is when he eats watermelon.

Waiter! Is there soup on the menu?
No, sir, I wiped it off.

Waiter, how long have you worked here?
Six months, Sir.
Well, it can't have been you who took my order.

What happened to Lady Godiva's horse when he realized that she wasn't wearing any clothes?
It made him shy.

Doctor, doctor, I think I'm a spoon.
Sit over there, please, and don't stir.

Doctor, doctor, my son's just swallowed some gunpowder!
Well, don't point him at me.

Doctor, doctor, I'm at death's door!
Don't worry, Mrs Jenkins. An operation will soon pull you through.

Doctor, doctor, Cuthbert keeps biting his nails!
That's not serious in a child.
But Cuthbert bites his toenails.

Nicky and Vicky were talking about a famous, very glamorous film star. "What do you think of her clothes?" asked Nicky.
"I'd say they were chosen to bring out the bust in her," replied Vicky.

Why did the farmer plow his field with a
steamroller?
Because he planned to grow mashed
potatoes.

Doctor, I keep stealing things. What can I
do?
Try to resist the temptation, but if you
can't, get me a new television.

Doctor: Good morning, Mrs Feather.
Haven't seen you for a long time.
Mrs Feather: I know, doctor. It's because
I've been ill.

How did the baker get an electric shock?
He stood on a bun and a current ran up his leg.

Do men always snore?
Only when they are asleep.

Doctor, doctor, how can I stop my cold going to my chest?
Tie a knot in your neck.

Doctor, doctor I keep losing my memory.
When did you first notice that?
When did I first notice what?

Some people say the school cook's cooking is out of this world.
Most pupils wish it was out of their stomachs.

Waiter, waiter, why is my apple pie all mashed up?
You did ask me to step on it, sir.

Did you hear about Lenny the Loafer? He is so lazy that he sticks his nose out of the window so that the wind will blow it for him.

What did the dinner lady say when the teacher told her off for putting her finger in his soup?
It's all right, it isn't hot.

Brian: How did you manage to get a black eye?
Bertie: You see that tree in the playground?
Brian: Yes.
Bertie: Well, I didn't.

Waiter, waiter, have you got frogs' legs?
No Sir, I always walk like this.

Ben, sniffing: Smells like UFO for dinner tonight, chaps.
Ken: What's UFO?
Ben: Unidentified Frying Objects.

Statistics say that one in three people is mentally ill. So check your friends and if two of them seem okay, you're the one.

Doctor, doctor, my wife thinks she's a duck.
You better bring her in to see me straight away.
I can't do that – she's already flown south for the winter.

What kind of beans do cannibals like best?
Human beans.

Did you hear about the two fat men who ran in the New York Marathon?
One ran in short bursts, the other in burst shorts!

Doctor, doctor, I think I'm invisible.
Who said that?

Did you hear about the dentist who
became a brain surgeon?
His drill slipped.

What do traffic wardens like for tea?
Traffic jam sandwiches.

Cannibal boy: I've brought a friend home
for dinner.
Cannibal mom: Put him in the fridge and
we'll have him tomorrow.

What is a dimple?
A pimple going the wrong way.

What happened to the man who put his
false teeth in backwards?
He ate himself!

What is the most popular food served at a
nudist camp?
Skinless sausages.

What's the best thing to put into a pizza?
Your teeth.

Ronald had broken a rib playing rugby. He went to the doctor, who asked how he was feeling. "I keep getting a stitch in my side," he replied.

"That's good," said the doctor. "It shows the bone is knitting."

Why did the old lady cover her mouth with her hands when she sneezed?
To catch her false teeth.

There was a fight in the fish-and-chip shop last night – a whole lot of fish got battered!

Doctor, doctor, I keep seeing double.
Take a seat, please.
Which one?

What kind of jokes does a chiropodist like?
Corny jokes.

Doctor, doctor, I think I've been bitten by a vampire.

Drink this glass of water.

Will it make me better?

No, but I'll be able to see if your neck leaks.

Which vegetable goes best with jacket potatoes?

Button mushrooms.

How can you tell an old person from a young person?

An old person can sing and brush their teeth at the same time.

Why are fried onions like a photocopying machine?
They keep repeating themselves.

My auntie has a sore throat. What should she do?
Take aunti-septic.

Who's stronger than a muscleman who can tear up a telephone directory?
Someone who can tear up a street.

Ben's new girlfriend uses such greasy lipstick that he has to sprinkle his face with sand to get a better grip.

Waiter: And how did you find your meat, sir?
Customer: Oh, I just lifted a potato and there it was.

Doctor, doctor! I'm becoming invisible!
Yes, I can see you're not all there.

What happens if you tell a psychiatrist you are schizophrenic?
He charges you double.

Waiter! What is that fly doing on my sorbet?
Learning to ski, sir.

A man who tests people's eyes is called an optimist.

The kidneys are infernal organs.

Why did the orange stop rolling down the hill?
It ran out of juice.

Doctor, doctor, I've only got fifty seconds to live.
Just sit over there a minute.

Did you hear about the girl who got
engaged to a chap and then found out he
had a wooden leg?
She broke it off, of course . . .

Doctor, doctor, it's wonderful! I feel like
my old self again.
In that case we'd better start a new
course of treatment.

My uncle's got a wooden leg.
That's nothing. My auntie has a wooden
chest.

How do you make gold soup?
Use fourteen carats.

Waiter, waiter, there's a bird in my soup.
That's all right, sir. It's bird-nest soup.

Waiter, waiter, this coffee tastes like mud.
I'm not surprised, sir, it was ground only a few minutes ago.

"I'm sorry," said the surgeon. "But I left a sponge in you when I operated last week."
"Oh," said the patient, "I was wondering why I was so thirsty all the time."

"Ugh! You smell terrible," said a doctor to a patient.

"That's odd," said the patient, "that's what the other doctor said."

"If you were told that by another doctor, why have you come to me?"

"Because I wanted a second opinion."

Trevor came rushing in to his dad.

"Dad," he puffed, "is it true that an apple a day keeps the doctor away?"

"That's what they say," said his dad.

"Well, give us an apple quick – I've just broken the doctor's window!"

"The sign says 'breakfast at any time,' so I want French toast during the Renaissance."

Jimmy was caught by his mother in the pantry. "And what do you think you're up to?" she asked furiously.

"I'm up to my seventh jelly tart," said Jimmy.

Now then, Deirdre, eat up all your greens like a good girl. They're good for your complexion, you know.

But I don't want to have a green complexion.

A man sat on a train chewing gum and staring vacantly into space, when suddenly an old woman sitting opposite said, "It's no good you talking to me, young man, I'm stone deaf!"

"The trouble is," said the entertainer to the psychiatrist, "that I can't sing; I can't dance; I can't tell jokes; I can't act; I can't play an instrument or juggle or do magic tricks or do anything!"

"Then why don't you give up show-business?"

"I can't – I'm a star!"

A tramp knocked on the back door of a house and asked for a bite to eat.

"Go away," said the lady of the house, "I never feed tramps."

"That's all right lady," said the tramp, "I'll feed myself."

Doctor, doctor! You've taken out my tonsils, my adenoids, my gall-bladder, my varicose veins and my appendix, but I still don't feel well.

That's quite enough out of you.

Little Jackie's mother was on the telephone to the boy's dentist.

"I don't understand it," she complained, "I thought his treatment would only cost me £10, but you've charged me £40."

"It is usually £10, madam," agreed the dentist, "but Jackie yelled so loudly that three of my other patients ran away!"

Three men were on trial, and the judge,
who had a terrible squint, said to the first,
"How do you plead?"
"Not guilty," said the second.
"I'm not talking to you," snapped the judge.
"I didn't say a word," said the third.

Fantasy
Figures

Did you hear about the monster who ate bits of metal every night?
It was his staple diet.

If a flying saucer is an aircraft, does that make a flying broomstick a witchcraft?

How do you get a ghost to lie perfectly flat?
You use a spirit level.

What do you call a ghost who only haunts the Town Hall?
The nightmayor.

Monster: Stick 'em down.

Ghost: Don't you mean, stick 'em up?

Monster: No wonder I'm not making much money in this business.

What do you call a skeleton who goes out in the snow and rain without a coat or an umbrella?

A numbskull.

What did the werewolf eat after he'd had his teeth taken out?

The dentist.

Mummy, mummy, what's a vampire?
Be quiet, dear, and drink your soup before it clots.

Why don't ghosts make good magicians?
You can see right through their tricks.

Did the bionic monster have a brother?
No, but he had lots of trans-sisters.

What did Frankenstein's monster say when he was struck by lightning?
"Thanks, I needed that."

What did E.T's mother say to him when he got home?
Where on Earth have you been?

What do you get if you cross a zombie with a boy scout?
A creature that scares old ladies across the road.

Ghost: Are you coming to my party?
Spook: Where is it?
Ghost: In the morgue – you know what they say, the morgue the merrier.

The ghost teacher was giving her pupils instructions on how to haunt a house properly. "Has everyone got the hang of walking through walls?" she asked. One little ghoul at the front of the class looked uncertain.

"Just watch the blackboard everyone," instructed the teacher, "and I'll go through it once more."

A monster decided to become a TV star, so he went to see an agent. "What do you do?" asked the agent.

"Bird impressions," said the monster.

"What kind of bird impressions?"

"I eat worms."

Igor: Only this morning Dr Frankenstein completed another amazing operation. He crossed an ostrich with a centipede.
Dracula: And what did he get?
Igor: We don't know – we haven't managed to catch it yet.

Did you hear about the monster who was known as Captain Kirk?
He had a left ear, a right ear and a final front ear.

Where does Dracula keep his savings?
In the blood bank.

Did you hear about the skeleton which was attacked by the dog?
It ran off with some bones and left him without a leg to stand on.

What did the werewolf write at the bottom of the letter?
Best vicious . . .

Woman in bed: Aaagh! Aaagh! A ghost just floated into my room!
Ghost: Don't worry, madam, I'm just passing through.

A monster walked into a shop selling dress fabrics and said, "I'd like six meters of pink satan for my wife."

"It's satin, sir, not satan," said the assistant. "Satan is something that looks like the devil."

"Oh," said the monster, "you know my wife?"

Teacher: What do you know about Lake Erie?
Rose: It's full of ghosts, Miss.

What happened when the werewolf met the five-headed monster?
It was love at first fright.

What airline do vampires travel on?
British Scareways.

What did the mother ghost say to the naughty baby ghost?
Spook when you're spooken to.

A horrible old witch surprised all her friends by announcing that she was going to get married. "But," said another old hag, "you always said men were stupid. And you vowed never to marry."
"Yes, I know," said the witch. "But I finally found one who asked me."

Why are vampires artistic?
They're good at drawing blood.

What did one skeleton say to the other?
If we had any guts we'd get out of here.

What happened when Dr Frankenstein
swallowed some uranium?
He got atomic ache.

Why did the wooden monsters stand in a
circle?
They were having a board meeting.

Dr Frankenstein decided to build an extension to his laboratory, so he crossed a cement mixer, a ghoul and a chicken. Now he's got a demon bricklayer.

What is even more invisible than the invisible ghost?
His shadow.

What's a skeleton?
Bones with the person off.

Why are Martians green?
Because they forgot to take their travel-sickness tablets.

What does Dracula say to his victims?
It's been nice gnawing you.

Why did Dracula eat strong peppermints?
Because he had bat breath.

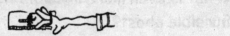

Ghost: Do you believe in the hereafter?
Phantom: Of course I do.
Ghost: Well, hereafter leave me alone.

Did you hear about the little spook who
couldn't sleep at night because his brother
kept telling him human stories?

Robot: I have to dry my feet carefully after a bath.
Monster: Why?
Robot: Otherwise I get rusty nails.

What kind of ghosts haunt hospitals?
Surgical spirits.

Two people went into a very dark, spooky cave. "I can't see a thing," said one.
"Hold my hand," said the other.
"All right." The first man reached out.
"Take off that horrible bristly glove first, though."
"But I'm not wearing a glove . . ."

Did you hear about the competition to find the laziest spook in the world? All the competitors were lined up on stage. "I've got a really nice, easy job for the laziest person here," said the organizer. "Will the laziest spook raise his hand?"
All the spooks put up their hands – except one.
"Why didn't you raise your hand?" asked the presenter.
"Too much trouble," yawned the spook!

A short, fat, hairy monster was waiting for a train and decided to while away the time by weighing himself on a machine on the station platform. Once he'd weighed himself he looked at the chart that indicated the ideal weight for each height. "Having any problems?" asked another passenger. "Are you overweight?"
"No," said the monster, "I'm just four feet too short."

Which day of the week do ghosts like best?
Moandays.

How do phantom hens dance?
Chick to chick.

What's the best way of avoiding infection
from biting ghosts?
Don't bite any ghosts.

What do you get if you try to take a
ghost's photograph?
Transparencies.

Who speaks at the ghosts' press
conference?
The spooksperson.

What is a ghost's favorite dessert?
Boo-berry pie with I-scream.

Why are ghosts invisible?
They wear see-through clothes.

Why is the graveyard such a noisy place?
Because of all the coffin!

What do you get if you cross a ghost with
a packet of crisps?
Snacks that go crunch in the night.

Which weight do ghosts box at?
Phantom weight.

Why did the witch put her broom in the washing machine?
She wanted a clean sweep.

What do you call a wizard from outer space?
A flying sorcerer.

What do you call a motor bike belonging to a witch?
A brrooooom stick.

Why do skeletons drink milk?
Because it's good for the bones.

Why was Dracula so happy at the races?
His horse won by a neck.

What do you get if you cross a vampire
with Al Capone?
A fangster!

How does a vampire enter his house?
Through the bat flap.

How does a vampire get through life with
only one fang?
He has to grin and bare it.

How did skeletons send each other letters
in the days of the Wild West?
By Bony Express.

What happens to a witch when she loses
her temper?
She flies off the handle.

Why do skeletons hate winter?
Because the cold goes right through them.

Why are skeletons usually so calm?
Nothing gets under their skin.

Word Play

Flash Harry gave his girlfriend a mink stole for her birthday. Well, it may not have been mink, but it's fairly certain it was stole.

What should you give short elves?
Elf-raising flour.

Why is classroom like an old car?
Because it's full of nuts, and has a crank at the front.

Where can you dance in California?
San Fran-disco.

What did the children do when there were rock cakes for lunch?
Took their pick.

1st undertaker: I've just been given the sack.
2nd undertaker: Why?
1st undertaker: I buried someone in the wrong place.
2nd undertaker: That was a grave mistake.

Did you hear about the florist who had two children?
One's a budding genius and the other's a blooming idiot.

How do we know that Rome was built at night?
Because all the books say it wasn't built in a day!

Ben's dad was building a pine bookcase, and Ben was watching and occasionally helping.
"What are the holes for?" Ben asked.
"They're knot holes," said his dad.
"What are they, then, if they're not holes?" said Ben.

Which two letters are rotten for your teeth?
D K.

What's the difference between a square peg in a round hole and a kilo of lard? One's a fat lot of good and the other's a good lot of fat!

What happens when business is slow at a medicine factory?
You can hear a cough drop.

What do you get if you cross a witch with an ice cube?
A cold spell.

Why do barbers make good drivers?
Because they know all the short cuts.

What did the "just married" spiders call their new home?
Newlywebs.

Sign on the school noticeboard: Guitar for sale, cheap, no strings attached.

Darren, at school dinner: I've just swallowed a bone.
Teacher: Are you choking?
Darren: No, I'm serious.

Girl: Shall I put the kettle on?
Boy: No, I think you look all right in the dress you're wearing.

What do you get if you cross a caretaker with a monk who smokes large cigars?
A caretaker with a bad habit.

Who carries a sack and bites people?
Santa Jaws

Sign outside the school caretaker's hut:
Will the person who took my ladder please return it, or further steps will be taken.

When George left school he was going to be a printer. All the teachers said he was the right type.

What's the difference between an iced lolly and the school bully?
You lick one, the others lick you.

Man to waiter: A pork chop, please, and make it lean.
Waiter: Certainly, Mr Smith, which way?

Why did the man go out and buy a set of tools?
Because everyone kept telling him he had a screw loose.

What's the difference between a nail and a boxer?
One gets knocked in, the other gets knocked out.

A pilot flying over the jungle was having trouble with his plane and decided to bail out before it crashed. So he got into his parachute, jumped, pulled the rip-cord, and drifted gently down to land. Unfortunately he landed right in a large cooking pot which a tribal chief was simmering gently over a fire. The chief looked at him, rubbed his eyes, looked again, and asked, "What's this flier doing in my soup?"

Two fleas were sitting on Robinson Crusoe's back as he lay on the beach in the sun. "Well, so long," said one to the other, "I'll see you on Friday."

Two fishermen were out in their boat one day when a hánd appeared in the ocean. "What's that?" asked the first fisherman. "It looks as if someone's drowning!" "Nonsense," said the second. "It was just a little wave."

What kind of bandage do people wear after heart surgery?
Ticker tape.

Did you hear about Mrs Dimwit's new baby? She thought babies should be pink, so she took this one to the doctor because it was a horrible yeller.

What happened to Ray when a ten-ton truck ran over him?
He became X-Ray.

Did you hear about the boy who got worried when his nose grew to eleven inches long?
He thought it might turn into a foot.

What do you do if you split your sides laughing?
Run until you get a stitch.

Do undertakers enjoy their job?
Of corpse they do.

Teacher: Didn't you know the bell had gone?
Silly Sue: I didn't take it, Miss.

Hil: Who was the fastest runner in history?
Bill: Adam. He was first in the human race.

Did you hear about the teacher who was trying to instil good table manners in her girls? She told them, "A well-brought-up girl never crumbles her bread or rolls in her soup."

Did you hear about the boy who was told to do 100 lines? He drew 100 cats on the paper. He thought the teacher had said "lions."

What's your handicrafts teacher like? She's a sew and sew.

What gets bigger the more you take away? A hole.

Why did the undertaker chop all his
corpses into little bits?
Because he liked them to rest in pieces.

Why was the insect thrown out of the
forest?
Because he was a litter bug.

What did the undertaker say to his
girlfriend?
Em-balmy about you.

What happened when the pussy swallowed
a penny?
There was money in the kitty.

A young lad was helping his dad with do-it-yourself jobs around the house. "You know, son," said the father, "you're just like lightning with that hammer."

"Fast, eh?" said the boy.

"Oh, no – you never strike in the same place twice."

What did the traffic light say to the motorist?

Don't look now, I'm changing.

What's the difference between a Peeping Tom and someone who's just got out of the bath?

One is rude and nosey. The other is nude and rosey.

Why did the lazy idiot apply for a job in a bakery?
He fancied a long loaf.

What's the difference between a sigh, a car and a monkey?
A sigh is oh dear. A car is too dear. A monkey is you, dear.

Was the carpenter's son a chip off the old block?

Do you serve women in this bar?
No sir, you have to bring your own.

What happens if you play table-tennis with a bad egg?
First it goes ping, then it goes pong.

Who is Wyatt Burp?
The sheriff with the repeater.

Why are school cooks cruel?
Because they batter fish and beat eggs.

What's a giant's favourite tale?
A tall story.

My sister thinks that a juggernaut is an empty beer mug.

What's the difference between a crossword expert, a greedy boy and a pot of glue?
A crossword expert is a good puzzler and the greedy boy's a pud guzzler. The pot of glue? Ah, that's where you get stuck.

What did the Eskimo children sing when their principal was leaving?
"Freeze a Jolly Good Fellow."

Ben's teacher regards Ben as a wonder child. He wonders whether he'll ever learn anything.

What's the difference between a kangaroo, a lumberjack and a bag of peanuts?
A kangaroo hops and chews and a lumberjack chops and hews.
Yes, but what's the bag of peanuts for?
For monkeys like you.

What do you get if you cross a burglar
with a concrete mixer?
A hardened criminal.

Who makes suits and eats spinach?
Popeye the Tailorman.

Where does Tarzan buy his clothes?
At a Jungle Sale.

Is this a second-hand shop?
Yes, sir.
Good. Can you fit one on my watch, please?

What is a mermaid?
A deep-she fish.

What kind of cans are there in Mexico?
Mexicans.

In the park this morning I was surrounded
by lions.
Lions! In the park?
Yes – dandelions!

Notice (in a new shop window): Don't go
elsewhere and be robbed – try us!

Jennifer: Are you coming to my party?
Sandra: No, I ain't going.
Jennifer: Now, you know what Miss told us.
Not ain't. It's I am not going, he is not
going, she is not going, they are not going.
Sandra: Blimey, ain't nobody going?

Passer-by (to fisherman): Is this river any
good for fish?
Fisherman: It must be. I can't get any of
them to leave it.

They're not going to grow bananas any
longer.
Really? Why not?
Because they're long enough already.

I wonder where I got that puncture?
Maybe it was at that last fork in the
road . . .

"Gosh, it's raining cats and dogs," said
Suzie looking out of the kitchen window.
"I know," said her mother who had just
come in. "I've just stepped in a poodle!"

A noise woke me up this morning.
What was that?
The crack of dawn.

Why is perfume obedient?
Because it is scent wherever it goes.

Which soldiers smell of salt and pepper?
Seasoned troopers.

A man with a newt on his shoulder walked
into a pub. "What do you call him?" asked
the barmaid. "Tiny," said the man.
"Why do you call him Tiny?"
"Because he's my newt!"

What do you get if you cross a nun and a
chicken?
A pecking order.

What does Luke Skywalker shave with?
A laser blade.

Which capital city cheats at exams?
Peking.

Why did the woman take a load of hay to bed?
To feed her nightmare.

What happened when the wheel was invented?
It caused a revolution.

Ivan: What are you reading?
Andrea: It's a book about electricity.
Ivan: Oh, current events?
Andrea: No, light reading.

How did Benjamin Franklin discover electricity?
It came to him in a flash.

Where do geologists go for entertainment?
To rock concerts.

Why is history the sweetest lesson?
Because it's full of dates.

What's wrong with this fish?
Long time, no sea.

What did the tie say to the hat?
You go on ahead and I'll hang around.

What did the picture say to the wall?
I've got you covered.

Why did the man take a pencil to bed?
To draw the curtains . . . I'd tell you
another joke about a pencil, but it hasn't
any point.

Why did the burglar take a shower?
He wanted to make a clean getaway.

Why do idiots eat biscuits?
Because they're crackers.

"What is your occupation?" asked the magistrate.
"I'm a locksmith, your honor."
"And what were you doing in the jeweller's shop at three in the morning when the police officers entered?"
"Making a bolt for the door!"

What do you call an American drawing?
Yankee Doodle.

A Dubliner was in court charged with parking his car in a restricted area. The judge asked if he had anything to say in his defense. "They shouldn't put up such misleading notices," said the Dubliner. "It said FINE FOR PARKING HERE."

What do you call an American with a lavatory on his head?
John.

What's the name for a short-legged tramp?
A low-down bum.

Why is it not safe to sleep on trains?
Because they run over sleepers.

Sign in a café: All drinking water in this
establishment has been personally passed
by the management.

Did you hear about the farmer's boy who
hated the country?
He went to the big city and got a job as a
shoe-shine boy, so the farmer made hay
while the son shone!

What did the Ancient Greeks shout when
Archimedes fell in a dung-heap?
You Reeka! You Reeka!

Did you her about the man who fell into an
upholstery machine?
He's fully recovered.

Numbskulls

A stupid glazier was examining a broken window. He looked at it for a while and then said: "It's worse than I thought. It's broken on both sides."

"How do you keep a stupid person happy for hours?"
"Give him a piece of paper with 'please turn over' written on both sides."

Did you hear about the man who hijacked a submarine?
He demanded a million dollars and a parachute.

When he received the end-of-term report Brenda's father went crazy. "This report is terrible," he said, "I'm not at all pleased with it."

"I told the teacher you wouldn't like it," said Brenda, "but he insisted on sending it just the same."

Why is the stupid red-headed boy like a biscuit?
Because he's a ginger nut.

Why do stupid people eat biscuits?
Because they're crackers.

Why did the robot act stupid?
Because he had a screw loose.

My mother is so stupid that she thinks a string quartet is four people playing tennis.

A man telephoned London Airport. "How long does it take to get to New York?"
"Just a minute."
"Thanks very much."

My friend is so stupid that he thinks twice before saying nothing.

Why did the stupid sailor grab a bar of soap when his ship sank?
He thought he could wash himself ashore.

Did you hear about the sailor that was discharged from the submarine service?
He was caught sleeping with the windows open.

An idiotic laborer was told by an equally idiotic foreman to dig a hole in the road.
"And what shall I do with the earth, sir?" asked the laborer.
"Don't be daft, man," he replied. "Just dig another hole and bury it."

Did you hear about the stupid motorist
who always drove his car in reverse?
It was because he knew the Highway Code
backward.

A stupid bank robber rushed into a bank,
pointed two fingers at the clerk and said:
"This is a muck up."
"Don't you mean a stick up?" asked the girl.
"No," said the robber, "it's a muck up. I've
forgotten my gun."

How do you confuse an idiot?
Give him two spades and ask him to take
his pick.

A stupid man spent the evening with some friends, but when the time came for him to leave, a terrific storm started with thunder, lightning and torrential rain. "You can't go home in this," said the host, "you'd better stay the night."

"That's very kind of you," said the man, "I'll just pop home and get my pajamas."

Doctor: And did you drink your medicine after your bath, Mrs Soap?
Mrs Soap: No, doctor. By the time I'd drunk the bath there wasn't room for medicine.

A mountaineer fell down a very deep crevasse, breaking both his arms. Another member of the party managed to lower a rope until it was just within reach of the man's head.

"Quick!" he shouted. "Get hold of the rope with your teeth and I'll pull you up." Inch by painful inch, the mountaineer was dragged back up the crevasse. When he only had two feet to go, his rescuer called out, "Are you all right?"

"Yes, aaaaaaaaaarrrrrrrrgggggghhh hhhh!" came the reply.

Waiter, waiter, this lobster's only got one claw.

It must have been in a fight, sir.

Then bring me the winner.

My sister is so stupid she thinks that aroma is someone who travels a lot.

Did you hear about the idiot who won the Tour de France?
He did a lap of honour.

An idiot decided to start a chicken farm so he bought a hundred chickens to start. A month later he returned to the dealer for another hundred chickens because all of the first lot had died. A month later he was back at the dealer's for another hundred chickens for the second lot had also died. "But I think I know where I'm going wrong," said the idiot. "I think I'm planting them too deep."

Did you hear about the idiotic karate champion who joined the army?
The first time he saluted, he nearly killed himself.

Sandra's mother said no young man in his right mind would take her to the school dance in her bikini, so she decided to go with her friend's stupid brother.

My big brother is such an idiot. The other day I saw him hitting himself on the head with a hammer. He was trying to make his head swell so his hat wouldn't fall over his eyes.

My sister is so dumb, she thinks that a buttress is a female goat.

How does an idiot call for his dog?
He puts two fingers in his mouth and then shouts Rover.

My friend is so stupid he thinks that an autograph is a chart showing sales figures for cars.

Why did the idiots' tug o' war team lose the match?
They pushed.

Teacher: You weren't at school last Friday, Robert. I heard you were out playing football.

Robert: That's not true, Sir. And I've got the cinema tickets to prove it.

Wally Woollynut was given the job of painting a flagpole but he didn't know how much paint he would need. "Lay it down and measure it," suggested a mate.

"That's no good," said Wally, "I need to know the height, not the length."

Did you hear about the idiot who had a new bath put in? The plumber said, "Would you like a plug for it?"
The idiot replied, "Oh, I didn't know it was electric."

Did you hear what Dumb Donald did when he offered to paint the garage for his dad in the summer holidays?
The instructions said "put on three coats," so he went in and put on his blazer, his raincoat and his duffel coat.

Did you hear about the utterly brainless monster who sat on the floor?
He fell off.

Did you hear about the stupid photographer?
He saved burned-out lightbulbs for use in his darkroom.

The math teacher and the English teacher went out for a quick pizza after school.
"How long will the pizzas be?" asked the math teacher.
"Sorry, Sir," replied the waiter, "we don't do long pizzas, just ordinary round ones."

Wilberforce Witherspoon saw a notice outside a police station which read: MAN WANTED FOR ROBBERY. So he went in and applied for the job!

My dad is stupid. He thinks a fjord is a Norwegian motor car.

Jimmy, how many more times must I tell you to come away from that biscuit barrel? No more, mom. It's empty.

What's red, runs on wheels and eats grass? A bus. I lied about the grass.

Did you hear about the village idiot buying bird seed?
He said he wanted to grow some birds.

I can't understand the critics saying that only an idiot would like that television program. I really enjoyed it.

Father: Would you like a pocket calculator for Christmas, son?
Danny: No thanks, Dad. I know how many pockets I've got.

At the scene of a bank raid the police sergeant came running up to his inspector and said, "He got away, sir!"
The inspector was furious. "But I told you to put a man on all the exits!" he roared. "How could he have got away?"
"He left by one of the entrances, sir!"

Did you hear about the stupid tap dancer?
He fell in the sink.

A stupid man was struggling out of his
house with a big table. His neighbor said to
him, "Hello, Harry. Where are you going
with that then?"
And Harry replied, "I'm taking it to the
draper's shop to have it measured for a
new tablecloth."

On their first evening in their new home the bride went in to the kitchen to fix the drinks. Five minutes later she came back into the living-room in tears.

"What's the matter, my angel?" asked her husband anxiously.

"Oh Derek!" she sobbed, "I put the ice cubes in hot water to wash them and now they've disappeared!"

A doctor had been attending a rich old man for some time, but it became apparent that the old chap had not long to live. Accordingly, the doctor advised his wealthy patient to put his affairs in order.

"Oh yes, I've done that," said the old gentleman. "I've only got to make my will. And do you know what I'm going to do with all my money? I'm going to leave it to the doctor who saves my life . . ."

Vincent, why have you got a sausage stuck behind your ear?
Eh? Oh no, I must have eaten my pencil for lunch!

A man rushed into the doctor's office, jumped on the doctor's back, and started screaming "One! Two! Three! Four!"
"Wait a minute!" yelled the doctor, struggling to free himself. "What do you think you're doing?"
"Well, doctor," said the eccentric man, "they did say I could count on you!"

Simple Simon was writing a geography essay. It began, "The people who live in Paris are called parasites . . ."

The criminal mastermind found one of his gang sawing the legs off his bed. "What are you doing that for?" demanded the crook boss.

"Only doing what you ordered," said the stupid thug. "You told me to lie low for a bit!"

A jeweler standing behind the counter of his shop was astounded to see a man come hurtling head-first through the window. "What on earth are you up to?" he demanded.

"I'm terribly sorry," said the man, "I forgot to let go of the brick!"

John kept pestering his parents to buy a video, but they said they couldn't afford one. So one day John came home clutching a package containing a brand-new video. "Wherever did you get the money to pay for that?" asked his father suspiciously. "It's all right, Dad," replied John, "I traded the TV in for it."

Classroom
Jokes

Alec turned up for football practice clutching a large broom.

"What's that for?" asked the coach.

"You said I was going to be sweeper today."

"Ann! Point out Australia for me on the map."

Ann went to the front of the class, picked up the pointer and showed the rest of the class where Australia was.

"Well done! Now, Alec! Can you tell us who discovered Australia?"

"Er . . . Ann, Miss?"

"Teacher is a bore!" was scrawled on the blackboard one day.

"I do not want to see that on my blackboard," he thundered when he saw it.

"Sorry, Sir! I didn't realize you wanted it kept secret."

"And what might your name be?" the school secretary asked the new boy.

"Well it might be Cornelius, but it's not. It's Sam."

What happens if there's a collision outside school?

There's usually a fight.

What happened to the baby chicken that misbehaved at school?
It was eggspelled.

Teacher: I was going to read you a story called "The Invasion of the Body Snatchers," but I've changed my mind.
Class: Oh why, Miss?
Teacher: Because we might get carried away.

"Ann," said the dancing mistress. "There are two things stopping you becoming the world's greatest ballerina?"
"What are they, Miss?" asked Ann.
"Your feet."

"I hope you're not one of those boys who sits and watches the school clock," said the principal to a new boy.

"No, Sir. I've got a digital watch that bleeps at half past three."

What's the definition of a school report? A poison pen letter from the principal.

Why did the soccer teacher give his team lighters? Because they kept losing all their matches.

What's the difference between school lunches and a bucket of fresh manure? School lunches are usually cold.

What's the longest piece of furniture in the school?
The multiplication table.

Did you hear about the cross-eyed teacher
who had no control over her pupils?

Miss Jones who teaches us maths,
Isn't a bundle of laughs.
For, sad to tell,
She doesn't half smell,
For she never seems to take any baths.

What do you get if you cross old potatoes
with lumpy stew?
School lunches.

Did you hear about the teacher who married the dairy maid?
It didn't last. They were like chalk and cheese.

"Why are you crying Amanda?" asked her teacher.
"'Cos Jenny's broken my new doll, Miss," she cried.
"How did she do that?"
"I hit her on the head with it."

Did you hear about the teacher who retired?
His class gave him an illuminated address.
They burned his house down.

Confucius he say: If teacher ask you question and you not know answer, mumble.

What did the arithmetic book say to the geometry book?
Boy! Do we have our problems!

"And what's your name?" the secretary asked the next new boy.
"Butter."
"I hope your first name's not Roland," smirked the secretary.
"No, Miss. It's Brendan."

"What's your first name?" the teacher asked a new boy.

It's Orson, Miss. I was named after Orson Welles, the film star."

"Just as well your last name's not Cart. Isn't it?"

"Yes Miss. It's Trapp."

Did you hear about the math teacher who fainted in class?

Everyone tried to bring her 2.

A little girl was next in line. "My name's Curtain," she said.

"I hope your first name's not Annette?"

"No. It's Velvet."

What's the difference between a boring teacher and a boring book?
You can shut the book up.

Teacher: That's the stupidest boy in the whole school.
Mother: That's my son.
Teacher: Oh! I'm so sorry.
Mother: You're sorry?

"Oh I'm sorry. I didn't realize you were her mother.
"I'm not. I'm her father actually! And she's my son!"

Typing teacher: Bob! Your work has certainly improved. There are only ten mistakes here.
Bob: Oh good, Miss.
Teacher: Now let's look at the second line, shall we?

A teacher in a country school received the following letter from the mother of one of his students:
Dear Teacher,
Please excuse Phil from school last week. His father was ill and the pig had to be fed.
Yours sincerely,

Why are art galleries like retirement homes for teachers?
Because they're both full of old masters.

It was sweltering hot outside. The teacher came into the classroom wiping his brow and said, "Ninety-two today. Ninety-two."
"Happy birthday to you. Happy birthday to you. . ." sang the class.

Did you hear about the brilliant geography teacher?
He had abroad knowledge of his subject.

"What's your father's occupation?" asked the school secretary on the first day of the new term.

"He's a conjurer, Miss," said the new boy.

"How interesting. What's his favourite trick?"

"He saws people in half."

"Golly! Now next question. Any brothers and sisters?"

"One half-brother and two half-sisters."

Billy's mother was called into the school one day by the principal.

"We're very worried about Billy," he said. "He goes round all day 'cluck, cluck, clucking'."

"That's right," said Billy's mother. "He thinks he's a chicken."

"Haven't you taken him to a psychiatrist?"

"Well we would, but we need the eggs."

Two elderly teachers were talking over old times and saying how much things had changed. "I mean," said the first, "I caught one of the boys kissing one of the girls yesterday."

"Extraordinary," said the second. "I didn't even kiss my wife before I married her, did you?"

"I can't remember. What was her maiden name?"

"Please Sir. There's something wrong with my stomach."

"Well button up your jacket and no one will notice."

"Now remember boys and girls," said the science teacher. "You can tell a tree's age by counting the rings in a cross section. One ring for each year."

Alec went home for tea and found a Swiss Roll on the table.

"I'm not eating that, Mum," he said. "It's five years old."

A warning to any young sinner,
Be you fat or perhaps even thinner.
If you do not repent,
To Hell you'll be sent.
With nothing to eat but school dinner.

Classroom Jokes

A mother was desperate to get her under-age daughter into kindergarten and was trying to impress the headmistress with the child's intellectual abilities. "She'll easily keep up with the others even though she is a year younger."
"Well," said the teacher doubtfully. "Could she prove it by saying something?"
"Certainly Miss," said the child.
"Something pertaining to your conversation, or something purely irrelevant?"

How do Religious Education teachers mark exams?
With spirit levels.

Teacher's strong; teacher's gentle.
Teacher's kind. And I am mental.

Why did the science teacher marry the
school cleaner?
Because she swept him off his feet.

Please Sir! Please Sir! Why do you keep me locked up in this cage?
Because you're the teacher's pet.

Teacher: Are you good at arithmetic?
Mary: Well, yes and no.
Teacher: What do you mean, yes and no?
Mary: Yes, I'm no good at arithmetic.

Why is a pencil the heaviest thing in your bag?
Because it's full of lead.

Mrs Jones: Well, Billy, how are you getting along with the trampolining?
Billy: Oh, up and down, you know.

Mandy: Our teacher went on a special banana diet.
Andy: Did she lose weight?
Mandy: No, but she couldn't half climb trees well!

Art teacher: What color would you paint the sun and the wind?
Brian: The sun rose, and the wind blue.

Teacher: Your books are a disgrace, Archibald. I don't see how anyone can possibly make as many mistakes in one day as you do.
Archibald: I get here early, Sir.

When is an English teacher like a judge?
When she hands out long sentences.

Geography teacher: What mineral do we import from America?
Daft Darren: Coca-Cola!

What's black and white and horrible?
A math examination paper.

What nickname did the police give to the
new blonde woman police officer?
A fair cop.

Kelly: Is God a doctor, Miss?
Teacher: In some ways, Kelly. Why do you
ask?
Kelly: Because the Bible says that the Lord
gave the tablets to Moses.

How can you tell when it's rabbit pie for
school dinner?
It has hares in it.

George knocked on the door of his friend's house. When his friend's mother answered he said: "Can Albert come out to play?"

"No," said the mother, "it's too cold."

"Well, then," said George "can his football come out to play?"

What is brown, hairy, wears dark glasses and carries a pile of exercise books?
A coconut disguised as a teacher.

Why did the teacher put corn in his shoes?
Because he had pigeon toes.

What do you call a deaf teacher?
Anything you like, he can't hear you.

How can a teacher double his money?
By folding it in half.

Teacher: What is an Indian's home called?
Andy: I don't know, Miss, but I know what
a little Indian's joke is called.
Teacher: Well, what is it called?
Andy: A Minihaha.

Girl: My teacher's a peach.
Mother: You mean she's sweet.
Girl: No, she has a heart of stone.

Headmaster: I've called you into my office, Peter, because I want to talk to you about two words I wish you wouldn't use so often. One is "great" and the other is "lousy." Peter: Certainly Sir. What are they?

Mother: How was your first day at school? Little Boy: OK, but I haven't got my present yet. Mother: What do you mean? Little Boy: Well the teacher gave me a chair, and said "Sit there for the present."

Teacher to pupil: How many thousand times have I told you not to exaggerate?

Did you hear about the schoolboy who just couldn't get to grips with decimals?
He couldn't see the point.

Father: Jennifer, I've had a letter from your principal. It seems you've been neglecting your appearance.
Jennifer: Dad?
Father: He says you haven't appeared in school all week.

Teacher: What happened to your homework?
Boy: I made it into a paper plane and someone hijacked it.

Tom: Why are you scratching your head?

Harry: I've got those arithmetic bugs again.

Tom: Arithmetic bugs – what are they?

Harry: Well, some people call them head lice.

Tom: Then why do you call them arithmetic bugs?

Harry: Because they add to my misery, subtract from my pleasure, divide my attention and multiply like crazy.

Teacher: What's the best way to pass this geometry test?

Boy: Knowing all the angles?

Teacher: You should have been here at nine o'clock.
Boy: Why? Did something happen?

Mother: What did you learn at school today?
Son: Not enough. I have to go back tomorrow.

Teacher: If I had ten flies on my desk, and I swatted one, how many flies would be left?
Girl: One – the dead one!

One unfortunate teacher started off a lesson with the following instruction, "I want you all to give me a list of the lower animals, starting with Georgina Clark . . ."

Music master: Brian, if "f" means forte, what does "ff" mean?
Brian: Eighty!

"Frank," said the weary math teacher, "if you had seven dollars in your pocket, and seven dollars in another pocket, what would you have?"
"Someone else's trousers on!"

Teacher: Martin, I've taught you everything I know, and you're still ignorant!

Teacher: Ford, you're late for school again. What is it this time?
Ford: I sprained my ankle, sir.
Teacher: That's a lame excuse.

Summer
Sensations

Where does an elephant go on holiday?
Tuscany.

What do you call a mosquito on holiday?
An itch-hiker.

What do you say to a hitch-hiking frog?
"Hop in!"

What do you get if you cross a frog with a ferry?
A hoppercraft.

How do toads travel?
By hoppercraft.

Which Cornish town is the favorite holiday spot for rodents?
Mousehole.

What do bees do if they want to use public transport?
Wait at a buzz stop.

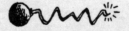

What happened when the cannibal crossed the Atlantic on the QE2?
He told the waiter to take the menu away and bring him the passenger list.

Where do witches go for their holidays?
Bat-lins.

Where did vampires go to first in
America?
New-fang-land.

Where do Chinese vampires come from?
Fanghai.

Where do zombies go for cruises?
The Deaditerranean.

What do demons have on holiday?
A devil of a time.

Where do ghosts go on holiday?
The Ghosta Brava.

Where do ghost trains stop?
At devil crossings.

Why are ghosts at their loudest in
August?
Because they're on their howlidays.

Which airway do ghouls fly with?
British Scareways.

Where do ghosts like to go on holiday?
Goole.

How did the rabbit get to Australia?
He flew by hareplane.

James: Do you know what nice people do on holiday?
John: No.
James: I didn't think you would.

Why couldn't the skeleton pay his bus fare?
Because he was skint.

Why did the bat miss the bus?
Because he hung around too long.

Why do you have to wait so long for a ghost train to come along?
They only run a skeleton service.

1st ghost: I died at Waterloo, you know.
2nd ghost: Really? Which platform?

1st witch: I'm going to France tomorrow.
2nd witch: Are you going by broom?
1st witch: No, by hoovercraft.

Did you hear about the ghost who learned to fly?
He was pleased to be back on terror-firma.

Where do ants go for their holidays?
Fr-ants.

How do fleas travel?
Itch-hiking.

What steps should you take if you see a dangerous yeti on your travels?
Very large ones.

What do Paddington Bear and Winnie the Pooh pack for their holidays?
The bear essentials.

The seaside resort we went to last year was so boring that one day the tide went out and never came back.

My girlfriend talks so much that when she goes on holiday, she has to spread suntan lotion on her tongue.

Boss: You're looking much better now, Reynolds. How's that pain?
Reynolds: She's away on a business trip.

Charlie was very nervous about going in a plane. "Do these planes crash often?" he asked the flight attendant.
"No," she smiled, "only once."

Nellie: Our teacher went to the West Indies for her holidays.
Kelly: Jamaica?
Nellie: No, she went of her own accord.

What can you see from the top of the
Eiffel Tower?
Quite an eyeful!

Which American city would a cow like to
visit?
Moo York.

Crossing the Atlantic in a Rowing Boat – by
Eva Lott

Summertime – by Theresa Greene

What did the sea say to the beach?
Nothing, it just waved.

Sarah: I'm going to sunbathe on my holiday. I love the sun.
Susie: Oh, so do I. I could lie in the sun all day and all night.

Darren went on a camping holiday with his family. "Did the tent leak?" asked his friend Sharon.
"Only when it rained," answered Darren.

Why did the principal like to take her main holiday in the spring?
She liked clean sheets on her bed.

Lizzie got a bad case of sunburn. When she complained how sore it was, her brother remarked, "Well, I guess you basked for it."

Passenger: Does this bus go to London?
Bus driver: No.
Passenger: But it says London on the front.
Bus driver: It says fish fingers on the side but we don't sell them!

In the summer holidays the math teacher collected information for a national opinion poll. But after a week she was sacked. Her vital statistics were wrong.

Mrs Broadbeam: Now, remember, children, travel is very good for you. It broadens the mind.
Sarah, muttering: If you're anything to go by, that's not all it broadens!

Pattie: We had a burglary last night, and they took everything except the soap and towels.
Peter: The dirty crooks.

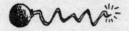

A pilot flying over the jungle was having trouble with his plane and decided to bail out before it crashed. So he got into his parachute, jumped, pulled the rip-cord, and drifted gently down to land. Unfortunately he landed right in a large cooking pot which a tribal chief was simmering gently over a fire. The chief looked at him, rubbed his eyes, looked again, and asked, "What's this flier doing in my soup?"

After years of traveling around the world in his search, the wicked Abanazar finally discovered the enchanted cave in which he believed lay the magic lamp which would make him millions. He stood before the boulders which sealed the cave, and uttered the magic words, "Open, sesame!" There was a silence, and then a ghostly voice from within moaned, "Open says-a-who?"

Why did the stupid pilot land his plane on a house?
Because the landing lights were on.

Harry was telling his friend about his holiday in Switzerland. His friend had never been to Switzerland, and asked, "What did you think of the scenery?"
"Oh, I couldn't see much," Harry admitted. "There were all those mountains in the way."

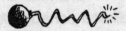

"Why did you come back early from your holidays?" one of Alec's friends asked him.
"Well, on the first day we were there one of the chickens died and that night we had chicken soup. The next day one of the pigs died and we had pork chops . . ."
"But why did you come back?"
"Well, on the third day the farmer's father-in-law died. What would you have done?"

What's green, has four legs and two trunks?
Two seasick tourists.

A woman just back from the United States was telling her friends about the trip. "When my husband first saw the Grand Canyon, his face dropped a mile," she said. "Why, was he disappointed with the view?" "No, he fell over the edge."

What is the best thing to take into the desert?
A thirst-aid kit.

A new porter at a Paris hotel was instructed by the manager that it was important to call the guests by their names, in order to make them feel welcome and that the easiest way to find out their name was to look at their luggage. Armed with this advice, the porter took two guests up to their rooms, put down their bags and said, "I hope you 'ave a very 'appy stay 'ere in Paris, Mr and Mrs Genuine Cow'ide."

What do you think of this suit? I had it made in Hong Kong.
Very nice, but what's that hump on the back?
Oh, that's the tailor. He's still working on it.

"I hope this plane doesn't travel faster than sound," said the old lady to the flight attendant.

"Why?"

"Because my friend and I want to talk, that's why."

Last time my wife and I traveled on the ferry from Newhaven to Dieppe, we had six meals.

Six meals for that short crossing?

Three down and three up.

A naughty child was irritating all the passengers on the flight from London to New York. At last one man could stand it no longer. "Hey kid," he shouted, "Why don't you go outside and play?"

The transatlantic liner was experiencing particularly heavy weather, and Mrs Ramsbottom wasn't feeling well.

"Would you care for some more supper, madam?" asked the steward.

"No thanks," replied the wretched passenger. "Just throw it overboard to save me the trouble."

First explorer: There's one thing about
Jenkinson.
Second explorer: What's that?
First explorer: He could go to
headhunters' country without any fear –
they'd have no interest in him.

Why is it not safe to sleep on trains?
Because they run over sleepers.

What is red outside, green and hairy
inside, and very crowded?
A bus full of gooseberries.

What's green and hairy and wears sunglasses?
A gooseberry on holiday.

What's sweet, sour, dangerous and travels?
Takeaway Kung food.

Where's a shark's favourite holiday destination?
Finland.

How do nits go on holidays?
British Hairways.

Why won't midfield players travel by
airplane?
In case they are put on the wing.

What's red and wobbles on top of sponge
cake and custard in the middle of Paris?
The Trifle Tower.

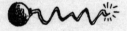

What makes the Tower of Pisa lean?
It doesn't eat much.

Kylie and Riley were talking about their forthcoming summer holidays. "Last year," said Kylie, "my brother and I took turns to bury each other in the sand."

"Yes, but what about this year?" interrupted Riley.

"I was coming to that," said Kylie. "This year we're going back to try to find him."

Local: Are you lost?
Stranger: No, I'm here. It's the bus station that's lost.

Letter from a travel agent: The flight you requested is fully booked but if someone falls out we'll let you know.

Notice at a railroad station: These toilets are out of order. Please use platform 6.

Louise: Did you hear about the stupid hitch-hiker?
Liza: No, what did he do?
Louise: He started his journey early so there wouldn't be so much traffic about.

Older brother: When I was a sailor I sailed both ways across the Atlantic without taking a bath.
Younger brother: I always said you were a dirty double crosser!

My Uncle Ben and Aunt Flo haven't had a
row for five years.
That's wonderful.
Not really. Uncle Ben lives in China.

What happens when a plane runs out of
fuel?
All the passengers get out to push.

Super
Slanders

What happens if you eat too much candy?
You take up two seats on the bus!

The school had given a concert and
Mrs Feather's son had played the piano.
She was very proud of him. She asked his
music teacher, "Do you think my Freddie
should take up the piano as a career?"
"No," replied the music teacher, "I think
he should put down the lid as a favour."

Ben's sister, Samantha, wanted to be an
actress when she left school.
"Is she pretty?" asked Bill.
"Let's just say she has a perfect face for
radio," answered Ben.

Nellie: I have an open mind.
Kelly: Yes, there's nothing in it.

Brian: How long can someone live without a brain?
Ryan: How old are you?

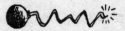

Lyn: I don't like soup.
Brian: I expect you can't get it to stay on the fork.

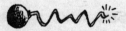

Trixie: When I die I'm going to leave my brain to science.
Tracey: I suppose every little helps.

Mick: Tim's gone to live in the city.
Nick: Why's that?
Mick: He'd read in the papers that the country was at war.

Man in clothes store: I'd like a blue shirt to match my eyes, please.
Sales clerk: I'm sorry, sir, we don't have any blue shirts. But we do have some soft hats that would match your head.

Jane: Do you ever do any gardening?
Wayne: Not often. Why?
Jane: You look as if you could do with some remedial weeding.

Jen: You look as if you'd find it hard to chew gum and walk at the same time.
Ken: And you look as if you'd find it hard to chew gum and breathe at the same time!

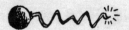

Barry: You're like uncultivated woodland.
Gary: Really?
Barry: Yes, totally dense.

Did you hear about the boy who was known as Fog?
He was thick and wet.

Holly: Do you ever find life boring?
Dolly: I didn't until I met you.

He's so stupid he thinks a cucumber is something you play pool with.

She's so stupid she thinks Christmas Eve is a tug of war.

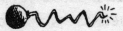

Charlie: Do you think I'm intelligent?
Chrissie: I'd like to say "yes" but my Mum says I must always tell the truth.

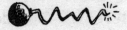

Emma: I'd like to say something nice about you as it's your birthday.
Gemma: Why don't you?
Emma: Because I can't think of a single thing to say!

Ivan: They say Ian has a dual personality.
Ivor: Let's hope the other one is brighter than this one!

Madge: Your body's quite well organized.
Martin: How do you mean?
Madge: The weakest part – your brain – is protected by the strongest – your thick skull!

Suresh: Whatever will Clive do when he leaves school? I can't see him being bright enough to get a job.
Sandra: He could always be a ventriloquist's dummy.

Hazel: I wonder what my IQ is?
Heather: Don't worry about it, it's nothing.

I always like to think the best of people, that's why I think of you as a complete idiot.

She has a mind of her own.
Of course she does. No one else would want it.

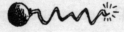

Did you hear someone has invented a coffin that just covers the head? It's for people like you who're dead from the neck up!

Bertie: You remind me of a Greek statue.
Gertie: Do you mean you think I'm beautiful?
Bertie: Yes, beautiful, but not all there.

Bennie: I've been told I must lose 5 kg of surplus fat.
Kenny: You could always cut off your head.

Cary: There's no point in telling you a joke with a double meaning.
Mary: Why not?
Cary: You wouldn't get either of them.

I'd like you to accept my opinion for what it's worth.
That means you owe me one cent.

My brother said he'd tell me everything he knows.
He must have been speechless.

Stella: Tracey has a ready wit.
Sheila: Perhaps she could let us know when it's ready!

Daniel: Being clever isn't everything.
Denzil: In your case it isn't anything.

My sister's going out with David.
Any girl who goes out with David must be able to appreciate the simpler things in life.

They say Margaret is a raving beauty.
You mean she's escaped from a loony bin?

In one way Julian is lucky. If he went out of his mind no one would notice the difference.

I feel sorry for your little mind – all alone in that great big head.

Jonathan ought to be a boxer. Someone might knock him conscious.

Why is your brother always flying off the handle?
Because he's got a screw loose.

Marie: Two heads are better than one.
Gary: In your case none might be better than one!

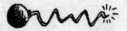

His speech started at 2 p.m. sharp.
And finished at 3 p.m. dull.

They call him Baby-face.
Does that mean he has a brain to match?

Brian: Let's play a game of wits.
Diane: No, Let's play something you can play too.

They say many doctors have examined her brain – but they can't find anything in it.

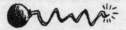

Don't let your mind wander. It's not strong enough to be allowed out on its own.

Jane: Do you like me?
Wayne: As girls go, you're fine. And the sooner you go the better!

Handsome Harry: Every time I walk past a girl she sighs.
Wisecracking William: With relief!

Freda: Boys whisper they love me.
Fred: Well, they wouldn't admit it out loud, would they?

Jerry: Is that a new perfume I smell?
Kerry: It is, and you do!

Laura: Whenever I go to my local shop the shopkeeper shakes my hand.

Lionel: I expect it's to make sure you don't put it in his till.

Bernie: Why have you given me this piece of rope?

Ernie: They say if you give someone enough rope they'll hang themselves!

Peter: My brother wants to work badly.

Anita: As I remember, he usually does.

Michael: It's hard for my sister to eat.

Maureen: Why?

Michael: She can't bear to stop talking.

Boss: Are you willing to do an honest day's work?

Secretary: Yes, as long as you give me an honest week's pay for it.

Son: How old are you, Dad?

Dad: Oh, around 35.

Son: I expect you've been around it a few times!

My brother's looking for a wife.

Trouble is, he can't find a woman who loves him as much as he loves himself.

He reminds me of a bowl of custard.

Yes, yellow and thick.

They say he works eight hours and sleeps eight hours.
Problem is, they're the same eight hours.

My dad once stopped a man ill-treating a donkey.
It was a case of brotherly love.

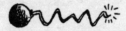

Gordon: My wallet's full of big bills.
Graham: All unpaid, I expect.

Jimmy: Is that lemonade OK?
Timmy: Yes. Why do you ask?
Jimmy: I just wondered if it was as sour as your face.

Lee: Our family's descended from royalty.
Dee: King Kong?

Anne: Do you think I look awful in this dress?
Dan: You could look worse – if I had better eyesight!

Mary: Do you think my sister's pretty?
Gary: Well, Let's just say if you pulled her pigtail she'd probably say "oink, oink."

Cheryl: They say I have an infectious laugh.
Meryl: In that case don't laugh near me!

Do you like my new baby sister? The stork brought her.
Hmm, it looks as if the stork dropped her on her head.

My sister went on a crash diet.
Is that why she looks a wreck?

My brother's on a seafood diet.
Really?
Yes, the more he sees food the more he eats.

Penny: No one could call your dad a quitter.
Kenny: No, he's been sacked from every job he's ever had.

Terry: When my mother was young she had a coming-out party.
Gerry: When they saw her they probably sent her back in again.

Winnie: I was cut out to be a genius.
Ginny: Pity no one put the pieces together properly.

I hear she was a war baby.
I'm not surprised – I expect her parents took one look at her and started fighting.

Does he have a big mouth?
Put it this way, he can sing a duet by himself.

Roy: They say ignorance is bliss.
Rita: Then you should be the happiest boy in the world.

Does your brother keep himself clean?
Oh, yes. He takes a bath every month
whether he needs one or not.

His left eye must be fascinating.
Why do you say that?
Because his right eye looks at it all the
time.

How can she be so fat? She eats like a
bird!
Yes, a vulture!

She once had a million-dollar figure.
Trouble is, inflation set in.

My boyfriend only has two faults –
everything he says and everything he does!

I hear he's a very careful person.
Well, he likes to economise on soap and
water.

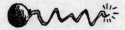

That girl looks like Helen Black.
She looks even worse in white.

Rich lady: That painting you did of me
doesn't do me justice.
Artist: It's not justice you want, it's
mercy!

New wife: Will you love me when I'm old and fat and ugly?
New husband: Of course I do!

She's so ugly that when a wasp stings her it shuts its eyes.

Bill and Gill make a perfect pair, don't they?
They certainly do. She's a pill and he's a headache.

They say she has a sharp tongue.
Yes, she can slice bread with it.

They say cleanliness is next to godliness.
With some people it's next to impossible!

Does he tell lies?
Let's just say his memory exaggerates.

Jane: I'll cook dinner. What would you like?
Shane: Good life insurance.

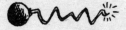

Harry's very good for other people's health.
Whenever they see him coming they go for a long walk!

Did you say he had a big mouth?
Put it this way, he's the only person I know
who can eat a banana sideways!

She could give a headache to an aspirin!

He's watching his weight.
Yes, watching it go up!

He's a light eater.
Yes, as soon as it's light he starts eating!

The last time I saw a face like yours I
threw it a banana.

Does he have big ears?
Let's just say he's very good at swatting flies.

Dickie: I hear the team's prospects are looking up.
Nicky: Oh good, are you leaving it then?

Bob had just missed a shot at goal, which meant the other team won. "I could kick myself," he groaned, as the players came off the pitch.
"Don't bother," said the captain, "you'd miss."

Golfer: Have you packed all my golf gear in the car?
Wife: Yes, dear: clubs, map, compass, emergency rations . . .

Boy: Have you got any custard left?
Canteen lady: Yes.
Boy: Well you shouldn't have made so much then.

Customer: Two soggy eggs on burnt toast, please.
Café owner: We can't serve that here, sir.
Customer: Why not, you did yesterday.

What happened when the umpire had a brain transplant?
The brain rejected him.

What did they call the crazy golfer?
A crack putt!

Canteen lady: Do you want more of this custard?
Boy: No thanks, I'm too young to die.

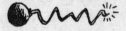

Despondent golfer: I'd move heaven and earth to get a better score.
Caddie: Concentrate on heaven, you've already moved enough earth!

Gloria: Boys fall in love with me at first sight.

Gordon: Yes, but when they take a second look they change their mind!

Harold: We should all try to fight air pollution.

Henry: You could start by stopping breathing.

Comedian: Do you find me entertaining?

Friend: I'd say you were too dumb to entertain a thought.

Boss: It would take ten men to fill my shoes.
Secretary, aside: It looks as if it took ten cows to make them.

Samantha: Don't I look gorgeous today?
Susannah: It's a treat for people to see you. After all, they have to pay to get into a freak show.

His clothes never go out of style – they look just as old-fashioned every year.

He's so stupid he probably couldn't spell "Anna" backwards.

He can't see further than the nose on his face.
No, but with his nose that's quite a distance.

Diner: Will the band play requests?
Waiter: Yes, sir. What would you like?
Diner: I'd like them to play cards.

I'm as pretty as a flower.
Yes, a cauliflower.

He asked me to tell him everything I know.
I bet you were speechless.

Words fail me.
I'd noticed you don't know how to use
them.

He thinks he's a big cheese.
I certainly have to hold my nose when I'm
near him.

He's such a whinger – if opportunity
knocked he'd complain about the noise.

He's the kind of boy girls dream about.
That's better than seeing him in broad
daylight.

You know how nurses slap babies when
they are born?
Yes.
Well, when you were born I reckon they
took one look and slapped your mother.

What do you think of Ada's looks?
I don't mind her looking, it's her face I
can't stand.

Monty: Does a mud pack help her complexion?
Bunty: It does for a few days, but then the mud falls off.

They say when the photographer took Jim's photograph he never developed it. Why?
He was afraid of being alone with it in a dark room.

The problem is, his facial features don't seem to understand the importance of being part of a team.

Do you think I have a good complexion?
Let's just say your face is almost as
smooth as a walnut.

Rosie: I like being tickled under the chin.
Josie: Which one?

Nigel has a Roman nose.
Yes, it's roamin' here, roamin
there . . .

I think she's quite old, don't you?
She has so many wrinkles on her forehead
she has to screw on her hat.

She's not very fat, is she?
No, she's got a really faminine look.
Her sister's skinny, too.
Yes, if she drinks tomato juice she looks like a thermometer.

Kylie: My uncle's just bought a pig.
Riley: But where will he keep it?
Kylie: Under the bed.
Riley: But what about the smell?
Kylie: The pig will just have to get used to it.

His death won't be listed under
"Obituaries," it will be under
"Neighbourhood Improvements."

She's so ugly that even spiders run away
when they see her.

Susie: I think a lot of people would go to
our principal's funeral.
Sally: Yes, to make sure she's dead!

Kate: I always speak my mind.
Kath: I'm surprised you've so much to say,
then.

Jimmy: Go and squirt lemon juice in your eyes.

Timmy: Whatever for?

Jimmy: It's the only way to make you smart.

You remind me of a toenail.

What do you mean?

The sooner you're cut down to size the better.

What's the difference between a bully and gravy?

Gravy's only thick some of the time.

Stella: You only have one use in life.
Ella: What's that?
Stella: Your face can cure hiccups!

Claud: What's the difference between you and a skunk?
Maud: I don't know.
Claud: You use a cheaper deodorant.

Darren: I'm so thirsty my tongue's hanging out.
Sharon: Is that your tongue? I thought it was a horrible spotted tie!

Bernie: What's the matter with your finger?
Ernie: I think I've got a splinter in it.
Bernie: Have you been scratching your head?

Angus: Have you been talking to yourself again?
Adam: Yes, how did you know?
Angus: You've got that bored look on your face.

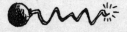

Glyn: You remind me of a builder's bottom.
Wyn: What do you mean?
Glyn: You're full of barefaced cheek!

Patty: What smells worse than a bad egg?
Mattie: I don't know.
Patty: You do!

What do you mean she eats like a bird?
She's enormous!
I expect she eats worms.

Gilly: Do you like my cottage pie?
Billy: No, it tastes as if you've left the drains in it.

Diner: This food isn't fit for a pig!
Waiter: I'll bring you some that is, sir.

I never forget a face – but in your case I'll make an exception.

Mr Black: I took my wife to the beauty parlor yesterday and I had to sit and wait all afternoon for her.
Mr White: Whatever was she having done?
Mr Black: Nothing – she just went for an estimate.

Mrs Brown: I took my son to the zoo yesterday.
Mrs Green: Did they accept him?

Hear about the stupid builder? He put a notice saying "Stop" on the top of his ladder.

Louise: What's the difference between you and a baby lamb?
Lionel: I don't know.
Louise: The lamb will one day be a sheep, but you'll always be a creep.

Andy: My dad's stronger than your dad.
Mandy: He must be after raising a dumb-bell like you!

Lesley: Did she really call you a creep?
Wesley: Yes. She said I was lower than the fluff in an earthworm's belly button, and if I was any more stupid, I'd have to be watered twice a week.

Cool
Connections

Darren, who was rather fond of Sharon, gave her a box of chocolates at break time on her birthday. "Here you are," he said, blushing, "sweets to the sweet."
"Oh, thanks," said Sharon. "Have a nut."

Hear about the woman who wanted to marry a ghost?
I can't think what possessed her.

Why did Frankenstein's monster squeeze his girlfriend to death?
He had a crush on her.

1st witch: I'm so unlucky.

2nd witch: Why?

1st witch: Last night I went to a party and met a handsome prince.

2nd witch: What's unlucky about that?

1st witch: When I kissed him he turned into a frog.

First boy: She had a beautiful pair of eyes, her skin had the glow of a peach, her cheeks were like apples and her lips like cherries – that's my girl.

Second boy: Sounds like a fruit salad to me.

Two men were having a drink together. One said, "I'd rather live with a vampire than with my wife."

"Why's that?" asked the other.

He said, "Because she's always trying to bite my head off."

A lady put a lonely hearts ad in the paper and had a reply which said, "I would love to meet you but I have to tell you that I am eight feet tall, covered in matted fur, with large fangs and slobbering lips. If you still want to meet me then I'll be under the clock in the market square at six o'clock next Saturday."

The lady replied, "I would be interested in meeting you but please will you wear a red carnation and carry a rolled-up newspaper so I can recognize you?"

I bet I could get you to forget about that horrible witch.

What horrible witch?

See, you've forgotten already.

The man tried to poison his wife again.
This time she lay on the floor shouting "Wretch, wretch, wretch!"
He said, "No, you retch – you took the poison."

Who is a vampire likely to fall in love with?
The girl necks door.

Me and the Wife – by Ian Shee.

Who was that I saw you with last night?
It was a girl from the school?
Teacher?
Didn't have to!

When Wally Witherspoon proposed to his girlfriend she said, "I love the simple things in life, Wally, but I don't want one of them for a husband."

A woman was in court charged with wounding her husband. "But madam, why did you stab him over 100 times?" asked the judge.
"Oh, your Honour," replied the defendant, "I didn't know how to switch off the electric carving knife."

Two girls were talking in the corridor.
"That boy over there is getting on my nerves," said Clarrie.
"But he's not even looking at you," replied Clara.
"That's what's getting on my nerves," retorted Clarrie.

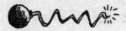

What did the two acrobats say when they got married?
We're head over heels in love!

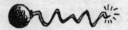

My girlfriend thinks I'm a great wit.
Well, she's half right.

A horrible old witch surprised all her friends by announcing that she was going to get married.

"But," said another old hag, "you always said men were stupid. And you vowed never to marry."

"Yes, I know," said the witch. "But I finally found one who asked me."

"The girl beside me in math is very clever," said Alec to his mother. "She's got enough brain for two."
"Perhaps you'd better think of marriage," said Mum.

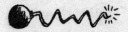

I can't understand why people say my girlfriend's legs look like matchsticks. They do look like sticks – but they certainly don't match.

Ben's new girlfriend uses such greasy lipstick that he has to sprinkle his face with sand to get a better grip.

"What's your new perfume called?" a young man asked his girlfriend.

"High Heaven," she replied.

"I asked what it was called, not what it smells to!"

"What do you do?" a young man asked the beautiful girl he was dancing with.

"I'm a nurse."

"I wish I could be ill and let you nurse me," he whispered in her ear.

"That would be miraculous. I work on the maternity ward."

I'm suffering from bad breath.

You should do something about it! I did. I just sent my wife to the dentist.

"What's the matter?" one man asked another.

"My wife left me when I was in the bath last night," sobbed the second man.

"She must have been waiting for years for the chance," replied the first.

Poor old Stephen sent his photograph off to a Lonely Hearts Club.

They sent it back saying that they weren't that lonely.

Freddie had persuaded Amanda to marry him, and was formally asking her father for his permission. "Sir," he said, "I would like to have your daughter for my wife."

"Why can't she get one of her own?" replied Amanda's father.

Why aren't you married?
I was born that way.

Mrs Jones and her little daughter Karen were outside the church watching all the comings and goings of a wedding. After the photographs had been taken, everyone had driven off to the reception and all the excitement was over, Karen said to her mother, "Why did the bride change her mind, Mummy?"

"How do you mean, change her mind?" asked Mrs Jones.

"Well," said the moppet, "she went into the church with one man and came out with another."

Why did you refuse to marry Richard, Tessa?
'Cos he said he would die if I didn't and I'm just curious.

My Peter keeps telling everyone he's going to marry the most beautiful girl in the world.
What a shame! And after all the time you've been engaged!

"But she's so young to get married," sobbed Diana's mother. "Only seventeen!"
"Try not to cry about it," said her husband soothingly. "Think of it not as losing a daughter but as gaining a bathroom."

"Doctor Sawbones speaking."
"Oh, doctor, my wife's just dislocated her jaw. Can you come over in, say, three or four weeks' time?"

A salesman was trying to persuade a housewife to buy a life insurance policy. "Just imagine, if your husband were to die," he said. "What would you get?"
"Oh, a sheepdog, I think," replied the wife. "They're so well-behaved."

My wife says that if I don't give up golf she'll leave me.
Say, that's tough, old man.
Yeah, I'm going to miss her.

Mrs Brown was always complaining about her husband. "If things go on like this I'll have to leave him," she moaned to Mrs Jenkins.
"Give him the soft-soap treatment," said Mrs Jenkins.
"I tried that," replied Mrs Brown, "it didn't work. He spotted it at the top of the stairs."

Mummy, mummy, why do you keep poking daddy in the ribs? If I don't, the fire will go out.

Mr Brown: I hate to tell you, but your wife just fell in the wishing well.
Mr Smith: It works!

My husband really embarrassed me yesterday. We were at the vicarage for tea and he drank his with his little finger sticking out.
But that's considered polite in some circles.
Not with the teabag hanging from it, it's not.

Wife to husband: I'll have you know I've got the face of a teenager!
Husband to wife: Then you should give it back, you're wearing it out.

Bill: What would it take to make you give me a kiss?
Gill: An anesthetic.

Harry: I've a soft spot for you.
Mary: Really?
Harry: Yes, in the middle of a bog!

James: I call my girlfriend Peach.
John: Because she's beautiful?
James: No, because she's got a heart of stone!

Romeo: I'd go to the end of the earth for you.
Juliet: Good. And when you get there, jump off!

My boyfriend only has two faults –
everything he says and everything he does!

They say he has a leaning towards blondes.
Yes, but they keep pushing him back.

Judge: Your first three wives died from eating poisonous mushrooms, and now your fourth wife has drowned in your swimming-pool. Isn't that all a bit odd?
Prisoner: Not really. She didn't like mushrooms.

I hear she doesn't care for a man's company.
Not unless he owns it.

My sister fell in love at second sight. When she first met him she didn't know how rich he was.

I got a gold watch for my girlfriend.
I wish I could make a trade like that!

What do you call pigs who live together?
Pen pals.

What's the best way to get rid of excess fat?
Divorce him.

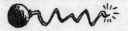

When my mom and dad got engaged she asked him if he would be giving her a ring.
He said, "Of course. What's your number?"

What will you do when you're as big as your dad?

Go on a diet!

Eskimo girl: There's something I'd like to give you.

Eskimo boy: What?

Eskimo girl: The cold shoulder.

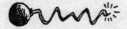

Wife: Did you like the food I cooked for you?

Husband: Let's just say it was a real swill dinner.

Barney: My girlfriend's cooking's like a good man.
Arnie: What do you mean?
Barney: Hard to keep down!

Wife: Did you really marry me because you'd heard my uncle had left me a fortune?
Husband: No, I'd have married you no matter who had left you a fortune.

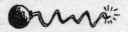

My wife is very dear to me.
Yes, I believe she costs you a fortune.

My husband's a millionaire.
He was a multi-millionaire before you married him.

My girlfriend loves nature.
That's very good of her, considering what nature has done for her!

How are you getting on with James?
Well, he's a bit dull until you get to know him.
And when you have got to know him you'll find he's a real bore!

He is pretty boring.
Yes, but he does have occasional moments of silence.

Husband: You took me for better or worse.
Wife: Yes, but I didn't think it would be this much worse.

Saul: My wife worships me.
Paul: Why do you think that?
Saul: She puts burnt offerings in front of me three times a day.

Wife: One more word from you and I'm going back to Mother!
Husband: Taxi!

They say he's her idol.
He certainly never does anything.

Myron: I can marry anyone I please!
Byron: But you don't please anyone!

Wife: We've been married 12 whole months.
Husband: Seems more like a year to me.

Wife: I've given you the best years of my life.
Husband: Are you asking me for a receipt?

Foreign visitor: And is this your most charming wife?
Husband: No, she's the only one I've got.

She talks so much he's never on speaking terms with her, just listening terms!

What do you call two elephants who leave their wedding on a bicycle?
Optimistic.

Can your husband cook?
Let's just say that yesterday he burned the salad.

Why do you call your girlfriend Treasure?
Because I wonder where she was dug up!

Kerry: My girlfriend's different from all other girls.
Terry: I bet she's different. She's the only girl around who'll go out with you!

How did Ann find out she'd married an elephant?
By the "E" on his pajamas.

When he told me he loved me he said he'd go through anything for me.
And has he?
So far he's only gone through my bank account.

Billy: Since I met you I haven't been able to eat or drink.
Tilly: Because you love me so much?
Billy: No, because I'm broke.

Young man: I've come to ask for your daughter's hand.
Father: You'll have to take the rest of her too or the deal's off.

Why do they call her an after-dinner speaker?
Because every time she speaks to a man she's after a dinner.

William: Bob's so suspicious, isn't he?
Wilfred: Yes. Even his eyes watch each other all the time.

Stan: You remind me of the sea.
Sue: Because I'm so wild and romantic?
Stan: No, because you make me sick!

Tom: Could you be happy with a boy like me?
Trish: Maybe, if you weren't around too often.

Jack: I was chosen by a computer as being an ideal boyfriend.
John: A computer's about the only thing that would have you as a boyfriend.

If we get married do you think you'll be able to live on my income?
Of course. But what will you live on?

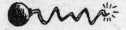

Mrs Rose: Where are you going to?
Mrs Thorn: The doctor's. I don't like the look of my husband.
Mrs Rose: Can I come with you? I can't stand the sight of mine!

Holly: How are you getting on with your advertisements for a husband? Have you had any replies?

Molly: Yes, lots. And they all say the same – take mine!

Clark: I'm not rich like Arwin, and I don't have a country estate like Brian or a Ferrari like Clive, but I love you and I want to marry you.

Clara: I love you too, but what did you say about Brian?

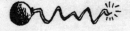

Husband: Let's go out tonight and have some fun.

Wife: Yes let's, but if you get home before I do, leave the light on please.

Brian: Why are you covered with scratches?
Byron: My girlfriend said it with flowers.
Brian: That sounds romantic.
Byron: It wasn't, she hit me round the head with a bunch of roses.

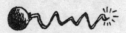

Samantha: Do you really love me?
Simon: Oh yes.
Samantha: Then whisper something soft and sweet in my ear.
Simon: Lemon meringue pie.

Wife: Today we're having Chicken Surprise.
Husband: What's the surprise?
Wife: You're cooking it.

303

Bridegroom: Will you really be able to put up with me for the rest of your life?
Bride: Of course, dear, you'll be out at work most of the time!

First man: Is your wife fat?
Second man: Put it this way, when we were married and I carried her across the threshold I had to make two trips.

Romeo: Will you come to the movies with me tonight?
Juliet: Oh no, I never go out with perfect strangers.
Romeo: Who says I'm perfect?

Juliet: Whisper those three little words
that will make my day.
Romeo: Go to hell!

They say she's been asked to get married
hundreds of times.
Really? Who by?
Her parents!

Ice
Breakers

Why did the cat put the letter "M" into the fridge?
Because it turns ice into mice.

Why is a polar bear cheap to have as a pet?
It lives on ice.

What was the fly doing on the ice cream?
Learning to ski.

What kind of money do yetis use?
Iced lolly.

What does a yeti eat for dinner?
Iceburgers.

How do ghosts like their drinks?
Ice ghoul.

What do you get if you cross a witch with an iceberg?
A cold spell.

Two witches lost their brooms and crash-landed on an iceberg.
"Do you think we'll be here long?" asked the first.
"No," said the second, "here comes the Titanic."

Waiter, waiter! What's this cockroach
doing on my ice cream sundae?
I think it's skiing downhill.

What happened when the ice monster had
a furious row with the zombie?
He gave him the cold shoulder.

What's the difference between an iced
lolly and the school bully?
You lick one, the others lick you.

What happened when the ice monster ate
a curry?
He blew his cool.

Simon: My girlfriend and I fell out last night. She wanted to go and watch ice-skating, but I wanted to go to the football match.
Peter: What was the ice-skating like?

What takes a lot of licks from a teacher without complaint?
An ice cream.

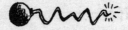

Wally: If frozen water is iced water, what is frozen ink?
Sally: Iced ink.

On their first evening in their new home the bride went into the kitchen to fix the drinks.

Five minutes she came back into the living-room in tears.

"What's the matter, my angel?" asked her husband anxiously.

"Oh Derek!" she sobbed, "I put the ice-cubes in hot water to wash them and they've disappeared!"

What did Tom get when he locked Jerry in the freezer?
Mice cubes.

Why did Ken keep his trumpet in the fridge?
Because he liked cool music.

A family of tortoises went into a café for some ice cream. They sat down and were about to start when Father Tortoise said, "I think its gong to rain, Junior, will you pop home and fetch my umbrella?"

So off went Junior for Father's umbrella, but three days later he still hadn't returned. "I think, dear," said Mother Tortoise to Father Tortoise, "that we had better eat Junior's ice cream before it melts."

And a voice from the door said, "If you do that I won't go."

Teacher: Order, children, order!
Daft Derek: Two chocolate ice creams and three orange lollipops, please.

What did the Eskimo schoolboy say to the Eskimo schoolgirl?
What's an ice girl like you doing in a place like this?

Ice Breakers

One very hot day an extremely small man went into a café, put his newspaper on a table and went to the counter. But on returning with a cup of tea he saw that his place had been taken by a huge, bearded, ferocious-looking man of some 300 pounds in weight, and six feet nine inches in height. "Excuse me," said the little man to the big man, "but you're sitting in my seat." "Oh yeah?" snarled the big man. "Prove it!" "Certainly. You're sitting on my ice cream."

Notice by a village pond: Beware! All of this ice is frozen.

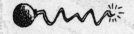

Why did Darren put his father in the freezer?
He wanted ice-cold pop.

How do you know if an elephant's been in your fridge?
There are footprints in the butter.

Why did the stupid witch keep her clothes in the fridge?
She liked to have something cool to slip into in the evening.

A woman went to the fridge to get some milk and all she found was a disembodied hand there.
It was all fingers and thumbs.

Cannibal Boy: I've brought a friend home for dinner.
Cannibal Mom: Put him in the fridge and we'll have him tomorrow.

What do you call the famous Italian artist who did his paintings sitting on the fridge?
Bottichilli.

Did you hear about the mad scientist who put dynamite in his fridge?
They say he blew his cool.

What stays hot in the fridge?
A hamburger with too much mustard on it.

What did the mayonnaise say to the fridge?
"Shut the door, I'm dressing."

What is brown one minute and white the next?
A rat in a deep-freeze.

Angela had to write down on her exam paper the name of a liquid that won't freeze, so she wrote "hot water."

What did the Eskimo children sing when one of their class was leaving school?
"Freeze a Jolly Good Fellow."

Why did the monster drink ten liters of anti-freeze?
So that he didn't have to buy a winter coat.

Why did the snowman call his dog Frost?
Because frost bites.

What's another way to describe a duck?
A chicken with snowshoes.

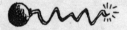

What exams do yetis take?
Snow levels.

Can the Abominable Snowman jump very high?
Hardly – he can only just clear his throat!

Teacher: Who knows what we mean by the Cold War?
Larry: Err, a snowball fight?

What kind of man doesn't like to sit in front of the fire?
An Abominable Snowman.

How do Abominable Snowmen feel when they melt?
Abominable!

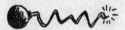

What do Abominable Snowmen call their offspring?
Chill-dren.

Where do Abominable Snowmen go to dance?
To snowballs.

What did one Abominable Snowman say to the other?
I'm afraid I just don't believe in people.

What is the Abominable Snowman's favorite book?
War and Frozen Peas.

What did the Abominable Snowman do after he had had his teeth pulled out?
He ate the dentist.

Why did the skeleton stay out in the snow all night?
He was a numbskull.

I Met An Abominable Snowman – by Anne Tarctic.

There was a young yeti from Gloucester
Whose granny and grandfather lost 'er.
Next day she was found
In the snow-covered ground
But they didn't know how to defrost her.

Doctor, doctor! I keep thinking I'm the Abominable Snowman.
Keep cool.

What does it mean if you have an elephant in your fridge?
He slept over, after the great party you had last night.

Did you hear about the woman who was so keen on road safety that she always wore white at night?
Last winter she was knocked down by a snow plow.

Billy: I never had a sled when I was a kid. We were too poor.
Milly, feeling sorry for him: What a shame! What did you do when it snowed?
Billy: Slid down the hills on my cousin.

Why was the snowman no good at playing in the big match?
He got cold feet.

Ted and Fred were enjoying themselves in the snow. "You can borrow my sled if you like," said Ted.
"Thanks," said Fred. "We'll share it, shall we?"
"Yes," said Ted. "I'll have it going downhill and you can have it going uphill."

Cooler
Cracks

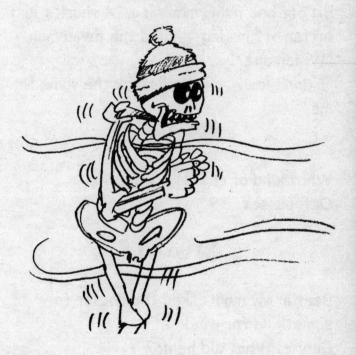

Two shark fishermen were sitting on the side of their boat just off the coast of Florida, cooling their feet in the sea. Suddenly an enormous shark swam up and bit off one fisherman's leg. "A shark's just bitten off my leg," yelled the fisherman. "Which one?"
"I don't know, all sharks look the same to me."

What kind of cats love water?
Octopusses.

Bertie: My mom asked the doctor for something for wind.
Gertie: What did he do?
Bertie: He gave her a kite.

Kevin: I'm really cool, you know.
Kieran: I always thought you were a cold fish.

Why is a football stadium cool?
It's full of fans.

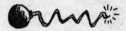

How do you know if your cat's got a bad cold?
He has cat-arrh.

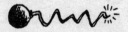

What do you give a pony with a cold?
Cough stirrup.

What does an octopus wear when it's cold?
A coat of arms.

What goes "hum-choo, hum-choo"?
A bee with a cold.

What's a cold, evil candle called?
The wicked wick of the north.

What kind of medicine does Dracula take for a cold?
Coffin medicine.

What happened to the zombie who had a bad cold?
He said, "I'm dead-up wid fuddy jokes aboud zondies."

Werewolf: Doctor, doctor, thank you so much for curing me.
Doctor: So you don't think you're a werewolf anymore?
Werewolf: Absolutely not, I'm quite clear now – see my nose is nice and cold.

Doctor, doctor! What would you take for this cold?
Make me an offer.

Why do skeletons hate winter?
Because the cold goes right through them.

Doctor, doctor! How can I stop my cold
going to my chest?
Tie a knot in your neck.

Doctor, doctor! I keep thinking I'm a dog
out in the cold.
Oh, stop whining.

What happened when the ice monster had
a furious row with the zombie?
He gave him the cold shoulder.

And what goes into the water pink and comes out blue?
A swimmer on a cold day!

What's hairy and damp and sits shivering at fairs?
A coconut with a cold.

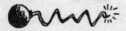

What's the difference between a bus driver and a cold?
One knows the stops; the other stops the nose.

What is hairy and coughs?
A coconut with a cold.

George knocked on the door of his friend's house.
When his friend's mother answered he said: "Can Albert come out to play?"
"No," said the mother, "it's too cold."
"Well, then," said George. "can his football come out to play?"

Geography teacher: What is the coldest place in the world?
Ann: Chile.

What can a schoolboy keep and give away at the same time?
A cold.

Did you hear about the snake with a bad cold?
No! Tell me about the snake with a bad cold.
She had to viper nose.

Why can you run faster when you've got a cold?
Because you have a racing pulse and a running nose.

Teacher: Matthew, what is the climate of New Zealand?

Matthew: Very cold, sir.

Teacher: Wrong.

Matthew: But sir! When they send us meat, it always arrives frozen!

Lady (to a tramp who's asked for a meal): Do you like cold prunes and custard?

Tramp: I love it, lady.

Lady: Well, call back later, it is very hot right now.

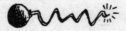

Young Horace was being taught how to box, but so far hadn't landed a single blow on his opponent.

"Don't worry, lad," said his teacher, "keep swinging – the draft might give him a cold."

Cooler Cracks

It was raining, and the goalie had let several goals through. As he came off the pitch he sniffed, and said, "I think I've caught a cold."
"I'm pleased to hear you can catch something," replied a fellow player.

It was a warm day and the baseball player kept missing his shots. After the match he sighed and said, "What couldn't I do with a long, cold drink?"
"Hit it?" inquired a fellow player.

Billy: Is your cold better?
Tilly: I've got a very bad head but I hope to shake it off soon.

He's so cold-blooded that if a mosquito bit him it would get pneumonia.

You're like a summer cold!
What do you mean?
It's impossible to get rid of you!

What animal with two humps can be found at the North Pole?
A lost camel.

Neddy: I've got a cold in the head.
Teddy: It must be the first time you've had anything in your head.

Cooler Cracks

How do sheep keep warm in winter?
Central bleating.

What likes to spend the summer in a fur coat and the winter in a swimsuit?
A moth.

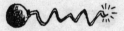

First cat: Where do fleas go in winter?
Second cat: Search me!

Waiter, waiter! There's a wasp in my pudding.
So that's where they go to in the winter.

Why don't vultures fly south in the winter?
Because they can't afford the air fare.

Why did the canoeist take a water pistol
with him?
So he could shoot the rapids.

What's thick, black, floats on water and
shouts "Knickers!"?
Crude oil.

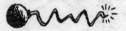

What do you get if you cross a bottle of
water with an electric eel?
A bit of a shock really!

What insect can fly underwater?
A bluebottle in a submarine

Teacher: Why do birds fly south in winter?
Jim: Because it's too far to walk.

What happens if you upset a cannibal?
You get into hot water.

What do you call a witch who likes the beach but is scared of the water?
A chicken sand-witch.

Why are vampire families so close?
Because blood is thicker than water.

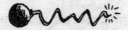

What do you call an alien starship that drips water?
A crying saucer.

"Now don't forget boys," the science teacher droned on, "If it wasn't for water we would never learn to swim. And if we'd never learned to swim, just think how many people would have drowned!"

That boy is so dirty, the only time he washes his ears is when he eats watermelon.

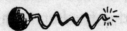

Did you hear about the idiot who made his chickens drink boiling water?
He thought they would lay hard-boiled eggs.

Teacher: Martin, put some more water in the fish tank.
Martin: But, Sir, they haven't drunk the water I gave them yesterday.

Mrs Twigg took her class on a nature ramble. They went past a large duck pond.
"Be careful not to fall in, children," she said, "the water's very deep."
"But it can't be, Miss," said Susie, "it only comes up to the middle of those ducks."

Why did the music student have a piano in the bathroom?
Because he was practicing Handel's Water Music.

Doctor, doctor! I think I've been bitten by a vampire.

Drink this glass of water.

Will it make me better?

No, but I'll be able to see if your neck leaks.

Anne: Ugh! The water in my glass is cloudy.

Dan, trying to impress his new girlfriend: It's all right, it's just the glass that hasn't been washed.

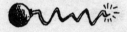

Daddy, daddy, can I have another glass of water please?

But that's the tenth one I've given you tonight.

Yes, but the baby's bedroom is still on fire.

When is the water in the shower room musical?
When it's piping hot.

Why did the teacher wear a lifejacket at night?
Because she liked sleeping on a waterbed, and couldn't swim!

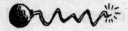

Which is the ghost's favorite stretch of water?
Lake Eerie.

Did you hear about the stupid water-polo player?
His horse drowned . . .

The food at the club dinner was awful. The soup tasted like dishwater, the fish was off, the meat was overcooked, and the vegetables were obviously old. The last straw for one member was the custard, which was thick and lumpy. "This meal is disgusting!" he roared. "And what's more, I'm going to bring it up at the annual board meeting next week!"

What is full of holes but can hold water?
A sponge.

A man in a swimming pool was on the very top diving board. He poised, lifted his arms, and was about to dive when the attendant came running up, shouting, "Don't dive – there's no water in that pool!" "That's all right," said the man. "I can't swim!"

Policeman: Why are you driving with a bucket of water on the passenger seat?
Motorist: So I can dip my headlights.

Jane: Have you noticed that your mother smells a bit funny these days?

Wayne: No. Why?

Jane: Well, your sister told me she was giving her a bottle of toilet water for her birthday.

Sign in a café: The management has personally passed all drinking water in this establishment.

He's so dumb that after he'd watched a gardening program on TV he started watering the light bulbs.

I hear he's a very careful person.
Well, he likes to economize on soap and water.

What happened to the yacht that sank in shark-infested waters?
It came back with a skeleton crew.

Why didn't the idiot go water-skiing when he was on holiday?
He couldn't find a sloping lake.

Notice by a river: When this sign is under water the towpath is flooded.

350

Mrs Green: How's your new house?
Mrs Brown: The roof needs mending. In last week's storm, rain was coming down the walls like water.

Bob: They say he has a waterproof voice.
Ted: What do you mean?
Bob: It can't be drowned out.

If we want to keep our heads above water we must keep our ears to the ground.

Ronnie: Why are you bathing in such dirty water?
Donnie: It wasn't dirty when I got in it.

How can I cure water on the knee?
Wear pumps.

Why do watermelons have to have a formal wedding?
Because they cant-elope.

Did you hear about the sailor that was discharged from the submarine service? He was caught sleeping with the windows open.

Wasps – while everyone runs a mile when they see one, why does it take hours for them to work out how to get out of a room, even after you've opened the window that they're standing on?

Doctor: You need new glasses.
Monster: How did you guess?
Doctor: I could tell the moment you walked through the window.

Doctor, doctor! I keep thinking I'm a moth.
So why did you come to see me?
Well, I saw the light in the window . . .

A wizard went to the doctor one day complaining of headaches. "It's because I live in the same room as two of my brothers," he said. "One of them has six goats and the other has four pigs and they all live in the room with us. The smell is terrible."

"Well couldn't you just open the windows?" asked the doctor.

"Certainly not," he replied, "my bats would fly out."

Art teacher: What color would you paint the sun and the wind?
Brian: The sun rose, and the wind blue.

How did the teacher forecast the weather with a piece of string?
She hung it up, and if it moved, she knew it was windy, and if it got wet, she knew it was raining.

Why does the Hound of the Baskervilles turn round and round before he lies down for the night?
Because he's the watchdog and he has to wind himself up.

Doctor, doctor! I think I'm Napoleon.
How long have you felt like this?
Since Waterloo.

Mr Jones met a neighbor carrying a front door. "Why are you carrying that, Tom?" asked Mr Jones.
"I've lost my key," replied Tom.
"Oh," said Mr Jones, "so how will you get in?"
"It's all right – I've left the window open."

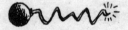

Who broke the window?
It was Andrew, Dad. He ducked when I threw a stone at him.

A jeweler standing behind the counter of his shop was astounded to see a man come hurtling head first through the window.
"What on earth are you up to?" he demanded.
"I'm terribly sorry," said the man, "I forgot to let go of the brick!"

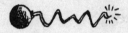

How do you cure a headache?
Put your head through a window, and the pane will disappear.

Sign in shop window: FOR SALE Pedigree bulldog. Housebroken. Eats anything. Very fond of children.

A man is in a prison cell with no windows and no doors; there are no holes in the ceiling or trapdoors in the floor, yet in the morning the wardens find him gone. How did he get out?

Through the doorway – there were no doors remember!

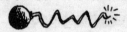

At a very posh wedding, one of the guests broke wind. The bridegroom was furious and rounded on the guilty party. "How dare you break wind in front of my wife?" he roared.

"Sorry," said the guest. "Was it her turn?"

"Gosh, it's raining cats and dogs," said
Suzie looking out of the kitchen window.
"I know," said her mother who had just
come in. "I've just stepped in a poodle!"

Dad, there's a man at the door collecting
for the new swimming pool.
Give him a glass of water!

Who was the first underwater spy?
James Pond.

What happened when the bell fell in the water?
It got wringing wet.

Don't look out of the window, Lavinia, people will think it's Hallowe'en.

Dylan: I take lots of exercise.
Duncan: I thought so. That's why you're so long-winded.

What happened to the man who couldn't tell putty from custard?
His windows fell out.

What happened to the man who couldn't tell the difference between putty and porridge?
His teeth stuck together and his windows fell out.

Father: George! Don't let the dog hang his head out of the window whilst driving!

Red Hot Funnies

What do you get if you pour hot water down a rabbit hole?
Hot cross bunnies!

It was so hot when we went on holiday last year that we had to take turns sitting in each other's shadow.

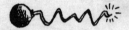

What do you get if you cross a snake with a hot dog?
A fangfurter.

What do frogs drink?
Hot croako.

What's white on the outside, green on the inside and comes with relish and onions?
A hot frog.

What happens if you eat a hot frog?
You croak in no time.

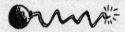

What is the proper name for the water otter?
A kettle.

What do witches ring for in a hotel?
B-room service.

1st cannibal: I don't know what to make of my husband.
2nd cannibal: How about a hotpot?

Hey, Waiter, you've got your thumb in my bowl of soup!
Don't worry, sir, the soup isn't hot.

It was sweltering hot outside. The teacher came into the classroom wiping his brow and said, "Ninety-two today. Ninety-two."
"Happy birthday to you. Happy birthday to you . . ." sang the class.

When the class went on a trip to the seaside, they stayed at a small hotel that advertised Bed and Board. The trouble was, they said afterwards, it was difficult to know which was the bed and which was the board.

What did the teacher say after spending thousands in the expensive hotel?
"I'm sorry to leave, now that I've almost bought the place."

Tarzan, coming home after a hard day's work: "Jane, it's a jungle out there."

A man arrived at a seaside hotel where he had made a reservation rather late at night. All the lights were out, so he knocked on the door. After a long time a light appeared in an upstairs window and a woman called out, "Who are you? What do you want?"

"I'm staying here."

"Stay there, then," she retorted, and slammed the window shut!

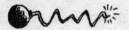

Teacher: I'd like a room, please.
Hotel receptionist: Single, Sir?
Teacher: Yes, but I am engaged.

There was a little old lady from a small town in America who had to go to Texas. She was amazed at the size of her hotel and her suite. She went into the huge café and said to the waitress, who took her order for a cup of coffee, that she had never before seen anything as big as the hotel or her suite. "Everything's big in Texas, ma'am," said the waitress. The coffee came in the biggest cup the old lady had ever seen. "I told you, ma'am that everything is big in Texas," said the waitress. On her way back to her suite, the old lady got lost in the vast corridors. She opened the door of a darkened room and fell into an enormous swimming pool. "Please!" she screamed. "Don't flush it!"

When we got to Benidorm the hotel was so full I had to sleep on a door across two tables. Was it comfortable?
Oh yes, but a bit drafty around the letter-box.

"Is my dinner hot?" asked the excessively late husband. "It should be," said his furious wife, "it's been on the fire since seven o'clock!"

Did you hear about the ghoul's favorite hotel?
It had running rot and mould in every room.

I was a waiter at the Hotel Splendiferous
for three months, but I had to leave on
account of the head waiter's nerves.
His nerves?
He couldn't stand the sound of breaking
crockery.

John: Do you feel like a cup of tea?
Don: Oh, yes.
John: You look like one, too – sloppy, hot
and wet!

There were two eggs boiling in a saucepan.
One said "Phew, it's hot in here."
The other said, "Wait till you get out, you'll
get your head bashed in."

Hotel porter: May I carry your bag, sir?
Hotel guest: That won't be necessary, my
wife is perfectly capable of walking.

What's green and served hot from the
oven?
An idiot's salad.

How do you stop someone who's been working out in the gym on a hot day from smelling?
Put a peg on his nose!

What's the hottest letter of the alphabet?
"B." It makes oil boil.

Did you hear about the two men who were cremated at the same time?
It was a dead heat.

What's the difference between Father Christmas and a warm dog?
Father Christmas wears a whole suit, a dog just pants.

What do you get if you cross an elephant with some locusts?
I'm not sure, but if they ever swarm – watch out!

How do mice celebrate when they move house?
With a mouse-warming party.

What did the drone say to the Queen Bee?
"Swarm in here isn't it?"

Why does a witch wear a pointed black
hat?
To keep her head warm.

Teacher: What do you think astronauts
wear to keep warm?
Girl: Apollo neck jumpers?

Bill: This loaf is nice and warm!
Tim: It should be – the cat's been sitting
on it all day!

Eddie was telling Freddie of his plans to make a lot of money.

"I intend to buy a dozen swarms of bees and every morning at dawn I'm going to let them into the park opposite my house to spend all the day making honey, while I relax."

"But the park doesn't open until nine o'clock," protested Freddie.

"I realize that," said Eddie, "but I know where there's a hole in the fence."

Darren was showing Sharon his holiday photos. She admired all the scenery and the people. Then Darren showed her a picture of him having a donkey ride on the beach. "Who's that on your back?" asked Sharon.

What was proved when the fat man was run over by a steamroller?
That he had a lot of guts.

Why did the farmer plow his field with a steamroller?
Because he planned to grow mashed potatoes.

"Your son is horribly spoiled," a woman said to a proud mother one day.
"How dare you!" retorted the second woman. "My son's a perfect little gentleman."
"I'm afraid you haven't seen what the steamroller's done to him!"

What's the difference between Frankenstein and boiled potatoes?
You can't mash Frankenstein.

1st cannibal: Come and have dinner in our hut tonight.
2nd cannibal: What are you having?
1st cannibal: Hard-boiled legs.

What do you call an English teacher, five feet tall, covered from head to toe in boils and totally bald?
Sir!

Psychiatrist: Well, what's your problem?
Patient: I prefer brown shoes to black shoes.
Psychiatrist: There's nothing wrong with that. Lots of people prefer brown shoes to black shoes. I do myself.
Patient: Really? How do you like yours – fried or boiled?

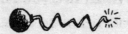

Wife, to husband: Boil the baby while I feed the potatoes, will you?

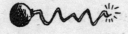

Heather: Help! I'm boiling!
Hyacinth: Oh, simmer down.

Giles: Can you lend me 10 pence? I want to phone a friend.
Miles: Here's 25 pence. Phone all your friends.

Doctor: Nurse, how is that little boy doing – the one who swallowed all those pennies?
Nurse: No change yet.